THE MIDNIGHT SNACK COOKBOOK

By Chris Hibbard

Illustrated by Mary Parks

SASSAFRAS PRESS
Evanston, Illinois 60204

THE MIDNIGHT SNACK COOKBOOK. Copyright © 1982 by Chris Hibbard and Sassafras Enterprises, Inc. All rights reserved. Printed in the United States of America. No part of this book may be used or reproduced in any manner whatsoever without the written permission of the publisher except in the case of brief quotations embodied in critical articles and reviews. For information address Sassafras Enterprises, Inc., P.O. Box 1366, Evanston, Illinois 60204.

LIBRARY OF CONGRESS CATALOG CARD NUMBER: 82-050380
ISBN NUMBER: 0-930528-04-2

First Printing First Edition   May, 1982
Second Printing   December, 1983

INTRODUCTION

Everyone loves a midnight snack. Some of us are satiated with a cookie and a glass of milk . . . usually because anything else seems too difficult to handle late at night.

The Midnight Snack Cookbook rises above the cookie and milk syndrome. Most of the recipes that follow are simple enough to prepare quickly (or ahead of time), yet are creative and interesting enough to satisfy the new "gourmet" food craving that has swept America. And, the recipes are presented with a relaxed feeling that will inspire even the laziest of midnight snackers.

Mary Parks, a free-lance artist and teacher, who so delightfully illustrated the book, lives in Batavia, Illinois, with her husband, Stan, and their newborn son, Brad.

Chris Hibbard is a school counselor currently working toward her doctorate degree in marriage and family counseling. She lives in Elburn, Illinois with her husband, Bob, and their dog, Molly. Her joy of cooking and creative approach have made this project fun to pursue.

Steven Schwab
Publisher

ACKNOWLEDGEMENTS

There are many memorable and novel experiences and relationships that evolve when doing a project such as the MIDNIGHT SNACK COOKBOOK. One of the most pleasant surprises was the discovery of the very talented people in "my own backyard" as these acknowledgements illustrate. This cookbook is unique because it is a reflection of the creative suggestions of a wide cross section of people who were all willing to contribute what they could in their area of expertise.

A very special thank you is in order for the encouragement and talents of . . .

STEVEN SCHWAB whose impeccable sense of timing, creativity and capitalization served as the impetus for writing a cookbook for the midnight snacker,

NANCY RUTHER POLAKOW for her confidence in choosing the writer and her direction throughout the book,

MARY PARKS whose brilliant artistry makes this book a visual delight,

RICH DREGER, our wine aficionado, for selecting just the right spirit to complement some of our very favorite "snacks",

Friends and family for being so generous with their suggestions, recipes, experience and sense of humor,

Molly, the family pet, for eagerly gobbling up all the "mistakes",

and to my husband, Bob - co-chef, co-dishwasher, and taste-tester, for joining in my ventures so good-naturedly and supportively.

I was fortunate to experience the fun, adventure and the support of good friends while writing this. To midnight snacking!

Chris Hibbard
May, 1982

TABLE OF CONTENTS

I. **ME AND MY SHADOW -** 9
   Recipes for the Lone Midnight Snacker

II. **FIRESIDE CHATS -** 25
    For Lovers only

III. **AFTER THE BALL IS OVER -** 39
     Suggestions for After Theater Entertaining

IV. **THE SUN ALSO RISES -** 57
    For that Late, Late Snack . . . or the Morning After

V. **HOW SWEET IT IS -** 69
   A Collection of Recipes for the Sweet Tooth

VI. **THE STUFF KIDS LOVE -** 83
    Recipes for Kids

VII. **INDEX -** 99

THE MIDNIGHT SNACK COOKBOOK

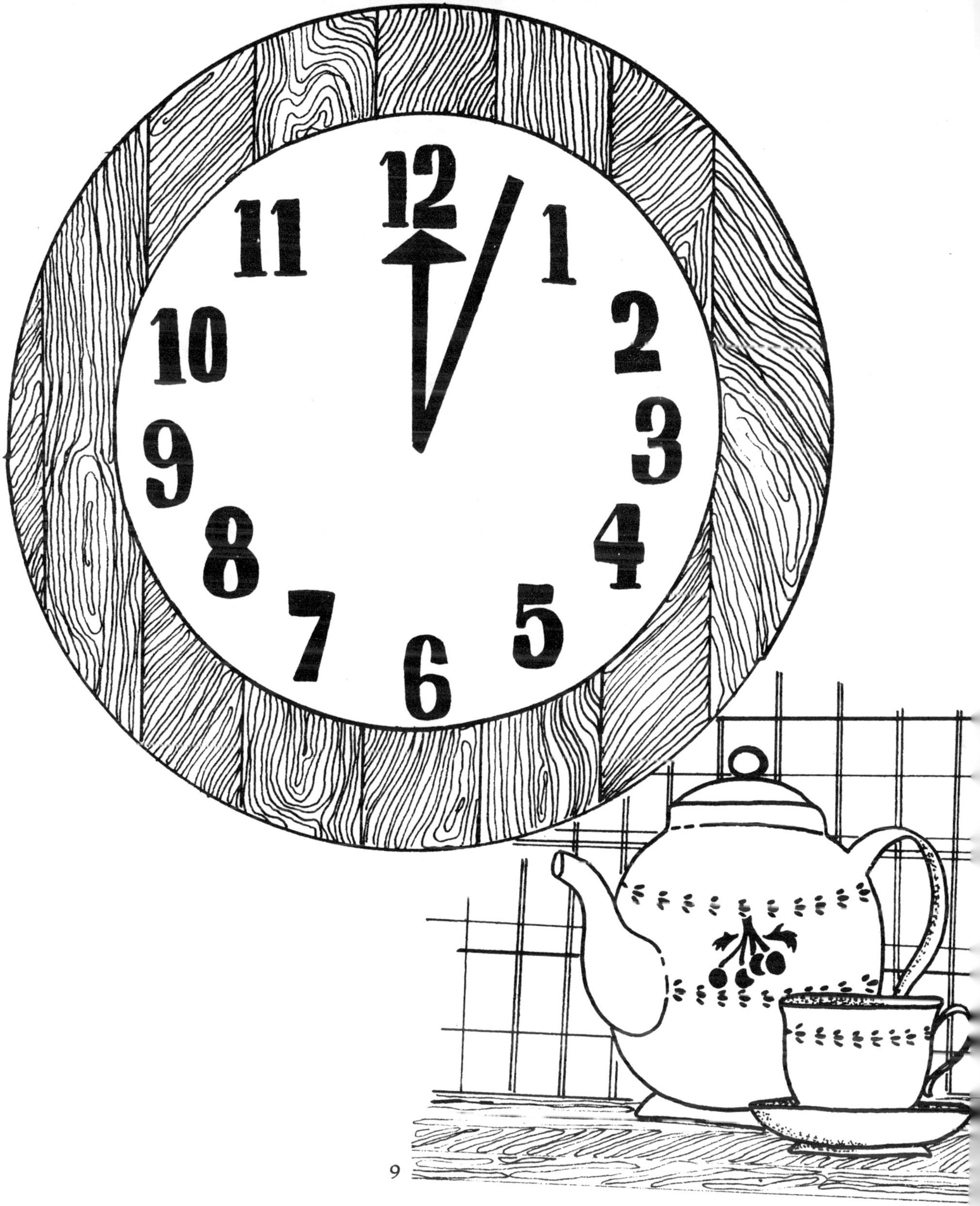

ME AND MY SHADOW

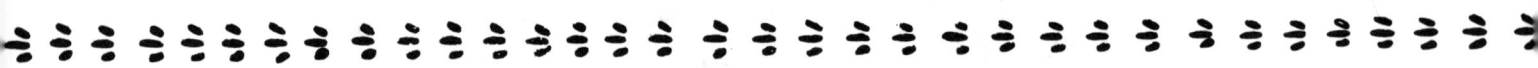

"Me and My Shadow" is a substitute for the creativity that just doesn't seem to be there at midnight. We asked friends and family what their favorite midnight snacks were and also came up with some new ideas in the process which use supper's leftovers as well as ingredients found in the cupboards and refrigerator.

Just so you'll be prepared for the next time hunger strikes, we've written a shopping list of things to have on hand . . . good insurance against opening the refrigerator and finding just a quart of milk and jar of mayonnaise!

Shopping List for the Lone Midnight Snacker

Pick and choose any or all:

Cans of: shrimp, crabmeat, chicken, sardines, tuna

English muffins, pumpernickel and wheat breads

Tomatoes, green onions, cucumbers, onions, avocados

Cheeses: cheddar, mozzarella, parmesan, cream cheese

Cans of Soup: cream of shrimp, cream of asparagus, cream of chicken, cream of celery, green pea

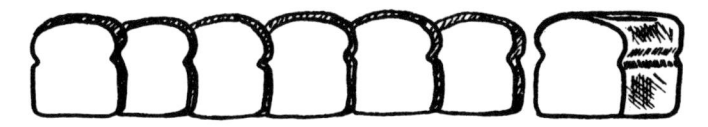

SANDWICH SUGGESTIONS

Bread...
makes an interesting sandwich if different varieties are combined in the same sandwich. Wheat, pumpernickel and white make an eye-catching triple decker sandwich. Sometimes, day old bread slices are better and allow for a more even distribution of spreaded fillings. If you prefer rolled sandwiches, fresh bread is the best choice.

Butter...
creams better when it is softened and allows for easier spreading. Never melt butter for sandwiches. Butter may also be kept at room temperature for an hour or so to soften. Butter prevents the sandwich from becoming soggy when a moist filling is used. One of the advantages of using soft butter is that it may be seasoned with herbs or combined with mayonnaise or cream for a change of pace.

Fillings...
are the creation of the cook's imagination (and whatever happens to be available in the pantry!). Use a variety of fillings on different layers in the same sandwich, such as egg salad on one layer, chicken salad on another layer and a slice of cheese on the third layer. Sliced fillings, such as meats and cheeses, should be sliced very thin. If you plan to keep the sandwich for any length of time, ingredients such as cucumbers, tomatoes, and lettuce should be added just before serving.

Prepare fillings ahead of time and store in jars in the refrigerator for the midnight snackers in your family.

DON'T GIVE ME ANY BOLOGNA
(alternatives to the coldcut drawer)

- mashed avocado, lemon juice, salt and garlic powder on melba toast
- jelly and chopped pecans on white bread
- mashed hard boiled eggs moistened with mayonnaise on whole wheat bread with any of the following:
    celery ... minced cooked liver ... bacon ... salmon ... ketchup ... ripe olives ... watercress ... 1 tsp. mustard ... leftover spinach ... anchovies ... small pieces of franks ... chopped pickle
- paper thin onions and Swiss cheese on bread, broiled just until the cheese melts
- cream cheese spread on banana bread
- tuna salad and mushrooms on an English muffin topped with a slice of cheddar cheese and broiled for 1 minute
- tomato and pepperoni on an English muffin topped with a slice of your favorite cheese and broiled just until cheese melts
- raisins and mayonnaise spread on whole wheat bread and topped with sliced bananas
- sliced cucumbers, mayonnaise and pepper on white bread
- cream cheese and crushed pineapple spread on bread or pound cake
- mashed sardines, salt and lemon juice on rye
- salmon salad (salmon, mayonnaise, onions and celery) on any kind of bread
- pimiento cream cheese, chili sauce and shrimp on bread

BLENDER GAZPACHO

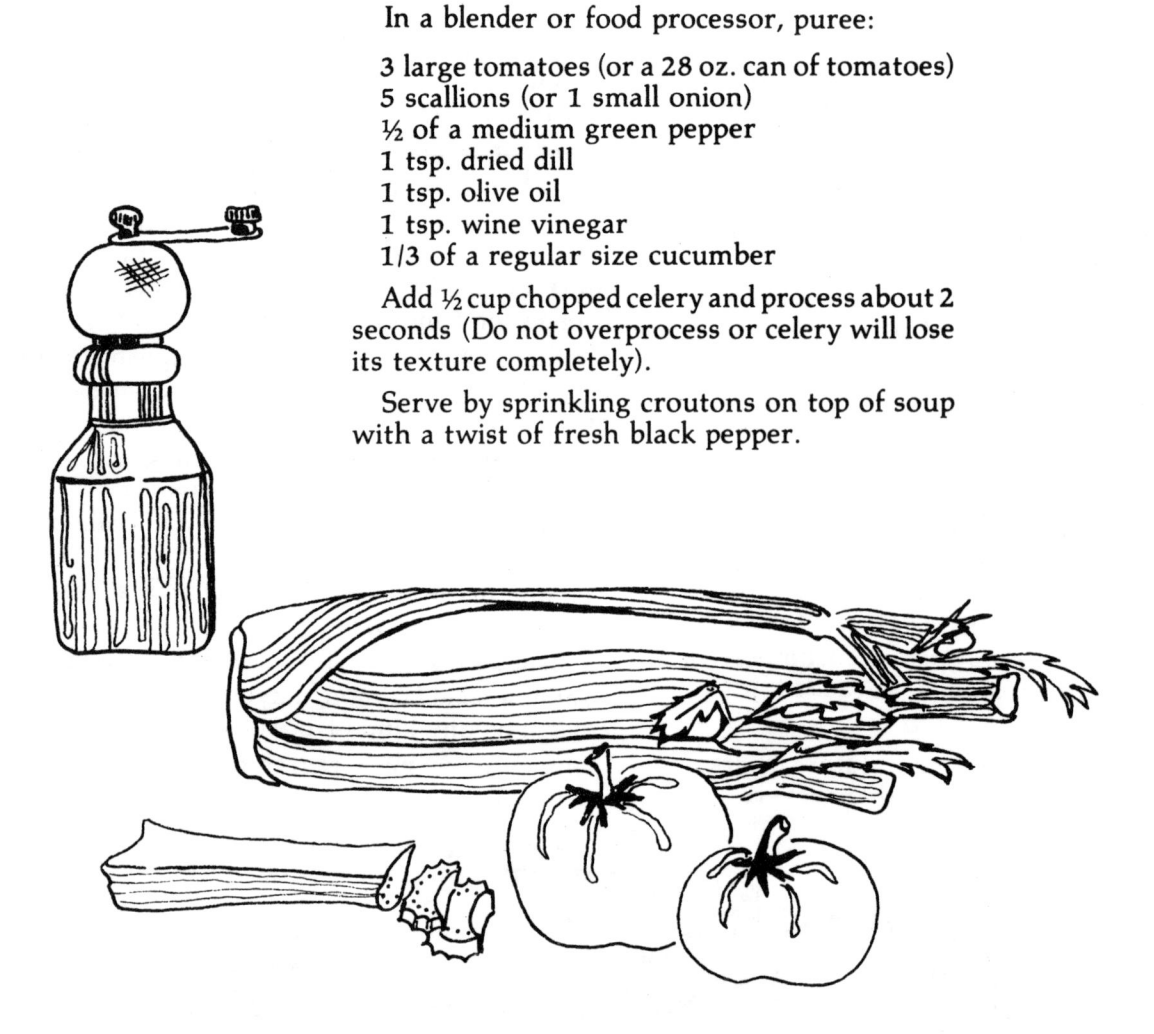

In a blender or food processor, puree:

3 large tomatoes (or a 28 oz. can of tomatoes)
5 scallions (or 1 small onion)
½ of a medium green pepper
1 tsp. dried dill
1 tsp. olive oil
1 tsp. wine vinegar
1/3 of a regular size cucumber

Add ½ cup chopped celery and process about 2 seconds (Do not overprocess or celery will lose its texture completely).

Serve by sprinkling croutons on top of soup with a twist of fresh black pepper.

HAVE YOU EVER TRIED PEANUT BUTTER...

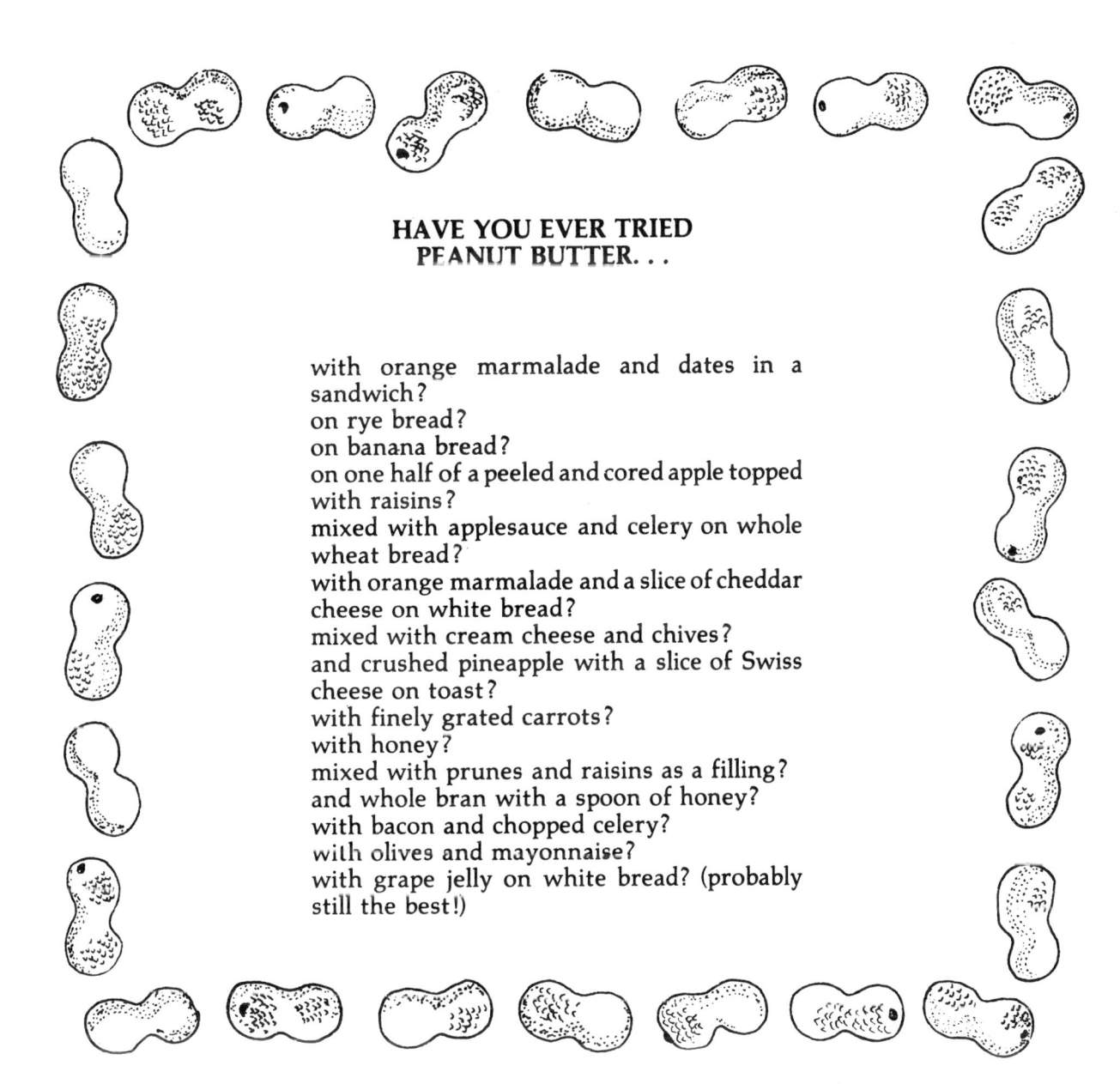

with orange marmalade and dates in a sandwich?
on rye bread?
on banana bread?
on one half of a peeled and cored apple topped with raisins?
mixed with applesauce and celery on whole wheat bread?
with orange marmalade and a slice of cheddar cheese on white bread?
mixed with cream cheese and chives?
and crushed pineapple with a slice of Swiss cheese on toast?
with finely grated carrots?
with honey?
mixed with prunes and raisins as a filling?
and whole bran with a spoon of honey?
with bacon and chopped celery?
with olives and mayonnaise?
with grape jelly on white bread? (probably still the best!)

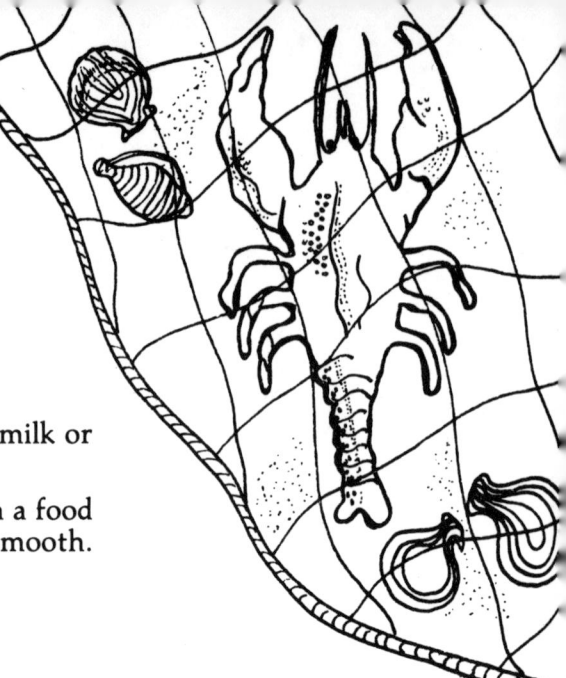

SEAFOOD BISQUE

A bisque is a cream soup made with milk or cream and butter.

Combine the following ingredients in a food processor or blender and process until smooth.

2 cups milk
1 T. flour
2 T. butter
1 tsp. salt
¼ cup chopped celery
2 T. minced onion

(Add celery and onion after processing if you prefer a chunkier bisque)

Heat over low heat until the mixture just starts to reach its boiling point. Then add one of the following ingredients to make your favorite variation.

Crab: Add 2/3 cup of cooked or canned crabmeat

Oyster: Add 4 raw oysters

Salmon: Add ½ cup of cooked or canned salmon

Shrimp: Add 2/3 cup of canned or fresh shrimp

Heat just until the seafood is warm. Serve with croutons or bread crumbs sprinkled over the top.

SESAME CHEESE ROUNDS

Preheat oven to 350°

1 English muffin, split in half
½ cup of shredded cheddar cheese
½ cup of shredded mozzarella cheese
1 T. grated parmesan cheese
½ tsp. onion powder (or more if desired)
mayonnaise
bacon bits
sesame seeds

Combine the cheddar, mozzarella and parmesan cheeses. Add the onion powder and moisten the mixture with mayonnaise (about 2 T.).

Place the mixture on each half of the English muffin. Sprinkle the top with bacon bits and sesame seeds.

Bake at 350° until the cheese melts (7-10 minutes). Serve while hot.

CHICKEN SALAD CONCOCTIONS

When you find yourself with some leftover chicken, try any of these combinations and place in jars, labeled, ready for late night snacking.

Chicken Salad Orientale

Blend the following and chill at least one hour before serving.

2 cups cooked chicken
3/4 cup chopped celery
3 green onions, chopped
1/4 cup chopped water chestnuts
1/2 tsp. ground ginger
1/2 tsp. salt
3/4 cup mayonnaise
1/4 cup slivered almonds

Chicken Salad Quick and Easy

Combine 1 cup chopped cooked chicken with 1/2 cup chopped celery and 1/2 cup chopped olives. Moisten with mayonnaise.

OR

Combine 1 cup chopped cooked chicken, 3 T. toasted almonds salt, pepper & 2 T. Thousand Island dressing.

CHICKEN

Grace's Hot Chicken Salad

2 cups cooked chicken
1 cup chopped celery
½ cup almonds, toasted
½ tsp. salt
½ tsp. MSG
2 tsp. grated onion
2 T. lemon juice
1 cup mayonnaise

Combine the above ingredients. Place in individual ramekins or baking shells. Sprinkle with grated American cheese and crushed potato chips. Bake at 450° for 10 minutes (until cheese melts.) and serve.

Chicken Salad ala Orange

Blend the following, adding mayonnaise to moisten.

2 cups cooked chicken
1 cup sliced celery
½ cup chopped walnuts
½ cup mandarin orange sections

WHAT'S LEFT ??

Try any of these sauces with cubes of supper's leftovers . . . pork tenderloin, roast beef, chicken . . . even steak.

Garlic Sauce

Process the following in a blender or food processor:
  4 cloves of garlic
  1/2 tsp. salt
  twist of pepper
  1 tsp. lemon juice
  2 raw egg yolks

Slowly add 1/3 cup of olive oil while machine is still running.

Snappy Tomato Sauce

Process the following ingredients in blender or food processor just until onion is chopped.
  1 cup catsup
  1 tsp. prepared mustard
  1 tsp. worcestershire sauce
  1 small onion
  dash of cayenne
  salt and pepper to taste

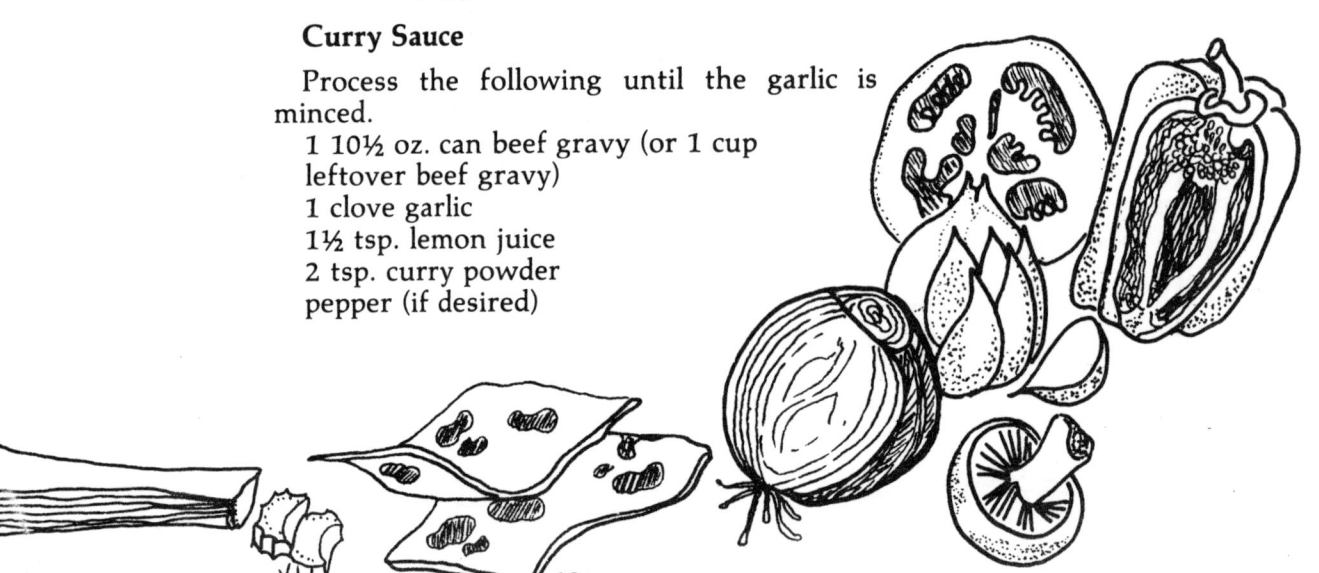

Curry Sauce

Process the following until the garlic is minced.
  1 10½ oz. can beef gravy (or 1 cup leftover beef gravy)
  1 clove garlic
  1½ tsp. lemon juice
  2 tsp. curry powder
  pepper (if desired)

STUFFED RABBIT STICKS

Try any of the following stuffed in a celery stick:

mashed avocado and bleu cheese
hard boiled egg mashed with mayonnaise, salt and pepper
cottage cheese and radish
grated cheddar cheese, mayonnaise and paprika
CREAM CHEESE and...
  nuts and pimiento
  stewed mashed apricots
  crushed beets
  chopped dates
  figs and honey
  olives and French dressing
  chopped watercress
  chopped sardines

Use only the tender white stalks of the celery plant that show no discoloration (inside stalks are best). Wash and leave tips of leaves on stalks or remove leaves from coarser stalks. Crisp in ice water and dry on paper towels before stuffing.

Use a pastry tube or knife to fill the celery grooves with stuffing.

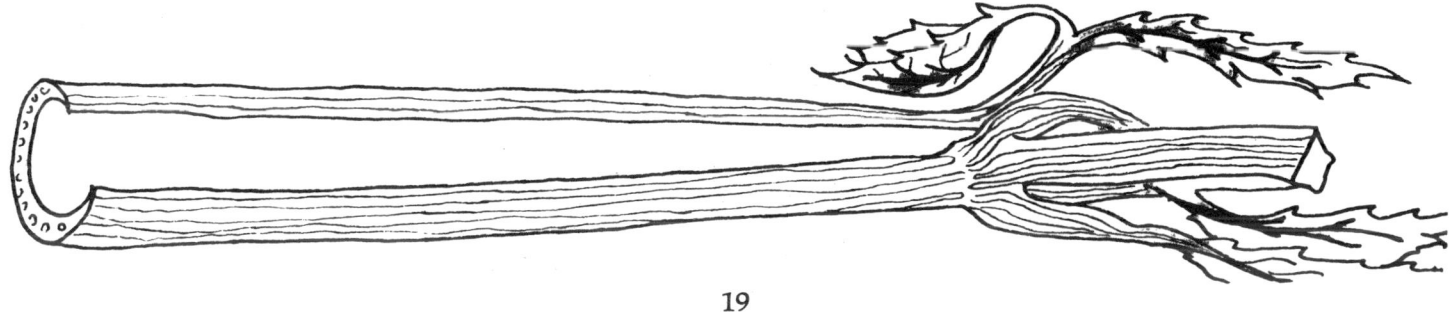

CANNED SOUP WIZARDRY

Shrimp Newberg
Combine:
　1 T. flour
　4 T. cream of
　　shrimp soup
and blend until
smooth. Add:
　remaining soup
　2 beaten egg yolks
Place on medium heat
and stir until
thickened. Add:
　1 can drained
shrimp and heat
until warm.
Serve with 2 T.
sherry sprinkled
over the top and
pour over toast,
English muffins or
miniature cream
puff shells (p. 45).

Chinese Egg Drop Soup
Heat:
　1 can chicken broth
until boiling. Slowly
pour in:
　1 well beaten egg
STIRRING RAPIDLY
with a fork until
the egg shreds. Serve.

Scotch Pea Soup
Combine:
　1 can green pea
　　soup
　2 cans of water
Stir well and add:
　1 can Scotch broth
Simmer 5 minutes
over medium heat.
Serve.

Bacon-Clam Chowder
Combine:
　1 can New England
　　clam chowder
　1 can cream of
　　celery soup
　1 can milk
　½ tsp. grated
　　onion (or
　　minced onion
　　flakes)
　1 T. parsley
　pinch of thyme

Heat to boiling and
simmer a few
minutes. Garnish
with 1 heaping T.
of bacon bits
(fresh or
prepared).

Creamiest Chicken Noodle Soup
Combine:
　1 can cream of
　　mushroom soup
　2 cans water
Heat, stirring
constantly. Blend in
　1 can chicken
　　noodle soup
Heat, but don't boil
and serve.

Cold Asparagus Soup
Combine:
　1 can cream of
　　asparagus soup
　1 can light cream
　　or milk
　A dash of
　　paprika
　　garlic salt
　　marjoram
　　fresh black pepper.
Chill and serve.

Chicken Corn Chowder
Combine:
　1 can cream of
　　chicken soup
　1 10 oz. pkg.
　　frozen cut corn
Cover and cook until
corn is tender.
Add bacon bits
and serve.

SOUP GARNISHES AND ACCOMPANIMENTS

The right garnish can lend the perfect touch to the most ordinary soup. You might try...

FOR CREAM SOUPS

salted whipped cream
minced parsley
toasted croutons (see below)
chopped pimiento
chopped chives
raw grated carrots
grated parmesan cheese
crumbled bacon
a dollop of sour cream

FOR CLEAR SOUPS

thin slices of lemon
avocado balls
celery rings or leaves
sauteed mushroom slices
julienned carrots
pea pods

FOR CHOWDERS

thin lemon slices
radish wheels
bacon bits

CROUTONS

Cut bread into ½ inch cubes.
Saute the bread in butter until brown OR spread the bread cubes on a buttered baking sheet and brown in a 350° oven for 10 to 15 minutes. For herbed croutons, sprinkle hot croutons with onion salt, garlic powder, fine herbs, parmesan cheese or just about anything that would flavor the bread.

ICE CREAM TOPPINGS FOR ONE

Try any of the following over a scoop or two of ice cream

- Toasted coconut and roasted almonds over vanilla ice cream

- Chocolate-Cherry Liqueur over chocolate ice cream for a "Black Forest" sundae.

- Marinate pineapple in creme de menthe and spoon over coconut, vanilla or peach ice cream.

- Marinate dark pitted cherries in cognac. Pour over vanilla ice cream.

- Heat prepared mincemeat (available in jars in the pie filling section) and pour over coffee, maple or vanilla ice cream.

- Crush peanut brittle (place in a small plastic bag and crush with a rolling pin) and roll a ball of hard ice cream in the crushed peanut brittle. Place in a dish and smother with hot fudge.

- Marinate orange slices in Triple Sec or Grand Marnier. Use the oranges over vanilla ice cream.

SAUCES (to make and have on hand)

Raspberry

Combine:
  1 pkg. frozen raspberries
  3 T. sugar
  1 T. lemon juice
and heat until melted.
Add: 1 tsp. cornstarch dissolved in 1 T. cold water.
Stirring constantly, bring to a boil. Remove from heat and add cognac to taste. Serve over your favorite ice cream or ice cream filled crepes.

Butterscotch

Combine:
  1½ cups brown sugar
  2/3 cup light corn syrup
  ½ cup water

Bring to a boil and cook until the mixture reaches 235°F Cool. Stir in ½ cup evaporated milk. Serve over ice cream or ice cream filled crepes. Top with chopped nuts.

TUTTI FRUITI

Banana Boats
Cut a peeled banana in half lengthwise. Spread one of the following on the banana evenly from tip to tip:

    Applesauce
    Apple Butter
    Honey
    Rum
    Brown Sugar
    Peanut Butter

Place in a baking dish and bake for about 8 minutes. Serve.

Gingered Pears
Place pear halves in a baking dish. Fill the center with honey and sprinkle lightly with ground ginger. Broil until bubbling hot (about 1 minute), and serve.

Spiced Oranges
Sprinkle orange slices with brown sugar and cinnamon. Put a cherry in the center of the slice and broil 3 to 4 minutes, and serve.

Fruit Ambrosia
Sprinkle 1/2 cup flaked coconut over a package of frozen mixed fruit. Let stand at room temperature until fruit is thawed. Mix and serve.

CANINE CHEWS (Strictly for dogs!)

At the sound of the refrigerator door opening, the family dog has probably followed you in search of his own midnight snack.

Preheat oven to 300°

Heat over low heat:
  2 cups of water or milk
  3 T. corn or vegetable oil
  2 squares unsweetened chocolate
  3 T. brown sugar

Stir just until chocolate melts. Pour this over a mixture of:
  3½ cups whole wheat flour
  2½ cups oatmeal

Stir until well mixed (dough will be very stiff). Pat out to ¼ inch thickness on a floured surface and cut with a "bone" cookie cutter (or one the shape of your dog if you can find one).

Bake for 1 hour and 10 minutes.

Note: These will spoil just as regular cookies because they do not have the preservatives that store bought dog biscuits have.

25

FIRESIDE CHATS

Create a mood with your choice of midnight snacks! "Fireside Chats" offers a variety of easy recipes to add even more to those quiet times together that seem too few.

Chicken liver pate with curry and a bottle of French red wine is perfect for a light snack after the movies, or a stuffed baked potato with ham and cheese sauce is a bit heartier for a late evening in front of the fire.

Have a drink while the fire gets started and enjoy a glass of wine with your fireside snack.

WHILE THE FIRE KINDLES

Vin Chaud for two

2 slices lemon
4 cloves
2 T. superfine sugar
2 cinnamon sticks
2 cups of Burgundy wine

Put 2 cloves in each lemon slice. Combine with sugar and cinnamon sticks in a saucepan. Place over medium heat and stir until the sugar has melted. Pour in the red wine and stir until very hot. Remove from the heat and pour into two mugs. Garnish with the lemon slice.

Daiquiri Frosts for two

Combine in a blender:
1 6 oz. can limeade frozen concentrate
6 oz. rum
8 ice cubes.

Blend for 10 seconds and pour into two large, frosted cocktail glasses.

Kir for two

4 ice cubes
1½ cups dry white wine
2 T. creme de cassis
2 strips lemon peel

Combine the ice, wine and creme de cassis. Stir gently. Twist a lemon peel over each glass and drop the peel in the glass. Fill each glass with the Kir.

Hot Buttered Rum for two

1 T. superfine sugar
2 cinnamon sticks
6 oz. rum
2 cups hot milk
2 T. unsalted butter
nutmeg

Heat the mugs by running under hot water and drying. Place ½ of the sugar, cinnamon and rum in each mug. Stir to dissolve the sugar. Pour 1 cup of hot milk in each mug and top with 1 T. butter. Garnish with nutmeg.

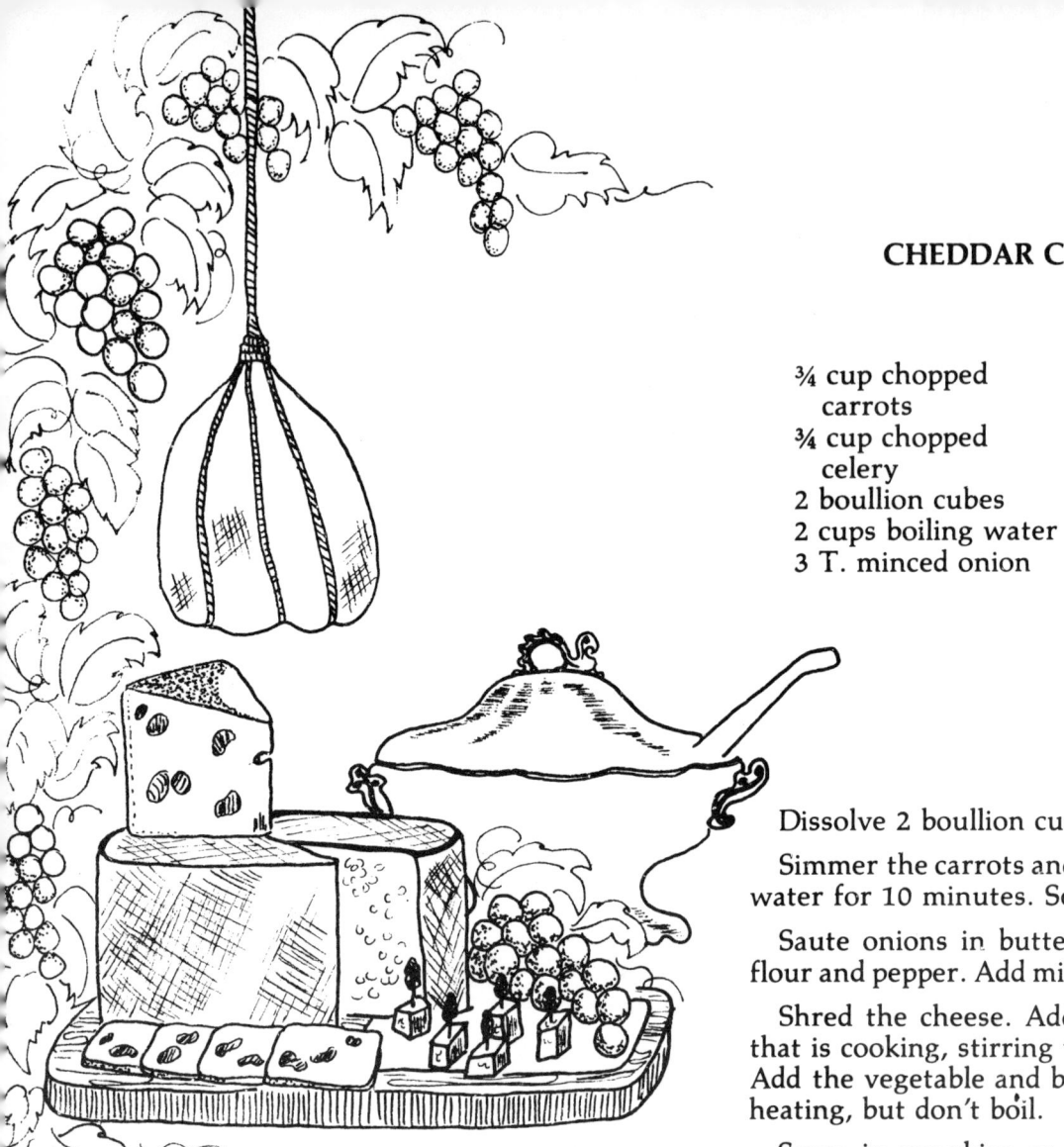

CHEDDAR CHEESE SOUP

¾ cup chopped carrots
¾ cup chopped celery
2 boullion cubes
2 cups boiling water
3 T. minced onion

3 T. butter
4½ T. flour
⅛ tsp. pepper
2 cups milk
½ lb. mild cheddar cheese.

Dissolve 2 boullion cubes in boiling water.

Simmer the carrots and celery in the boullion water for 10 minutes. Set aside.

Saute onions in butter until tender. Stir in flour and pepper. Add milk and cook until thick.

Shred the cheese. Add to the milk mixture that is cooking, stirring with a wooden spoon. Add the vegetable and boullion mixture. Keep heating, but don't boil.

Serve in ramekins or onion soup casseroles and top with fresh chives (if available) or freeze dried chives.

Wine Suggestion:
French red Burgundy

TOMATO BREAD

Preheat oven to 350°
1 loaf of French bread, split lengthwise
½ lb. mozzarella cheese
2 large tomatoes
Italian seasoning
butter

Butter the bread, covering the whole surface of each half.

Slice the cheese (thin) and place on the bread. Slice the tomatoes and lay on the cheese. Sprinkle tomatoes with Italian seasoning.

Place bread on a baking sheet or baking stone and bake at 350° for 10 minutes - just until the cheese melts.

For serving, slice diagonally into 1 inch pieces and place in a basket.

Wine Suggestion:
California red wine

FETTUCINI ALFREDO

½ of an 8 oz. bag of fettucini
 (thin egg noodles)
2 T. butter
½ cup freshly grated parmesan cheese
½ cup heavy cream
a few twists of black pepper
salt to taste

Cook fettucini according to package directions. Drain.

Toss the noodles with the butter, parmesan cheese and black pepper.

Heat the cream just until it becomes warm, and fold it into the noodle mixture. Toss so noodles are evenly coated.

Serve fettucini in two ramekins or au gratin dishes and garnish with more freshly grated parmesan cheese. Serve with a slice of crusty French bread.

Wine Suggestion:
Dry California White Riesling

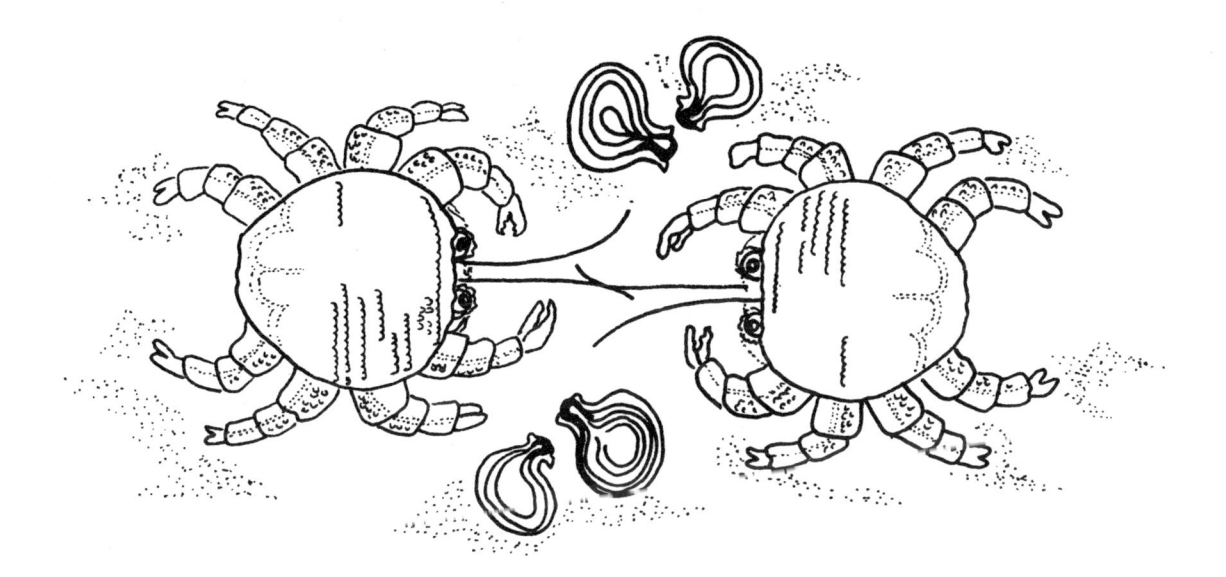

CRABMEAT ala NANCY

Preheat oven to 350°

1 package "party rolls" (come in a foil pan)
½ stick butter
4 oz. jar of pasteurized cheese food
(or 4 oz. mild cheddar cheese)
3 oz. canned crabmeat

Melt the butter. Add the cheese and stir until melted. Add the crabmeat, blend and heat until the crabmeat has blended with the cheese.

Turn the rolls **upside down** in the foil pan and pour the cheese mixture over the wrong side of the rolls.

Bake 5 to 8 minutes until the cheese is bubbly and the rolls are heated through. Cut the rolls into squares and serve on a platter.

Makes about 20 small pieces.

Wine Suggestion:
German Riesling

HOT CRABMEAT DIP

Preheat oven to 350°

Combine the following ingredients in a saucepan:

1 8 oz. pkg. cream cheese
2 6 oz. cans of crabmeat
2 T. chopped onion
1 T. milk
½ tsp. horseradish
¼ tsp. salt
¼ tsp. pepper
1/3 cup slivered almonds.

Heat all of the ingredients (except the almonds). When cheese has melted and mixture is smooth, pour into a chafing dish. Garnish with the almonds.

Bake in oven at 350° for 15 minutes.

Remove from oven and serve with small slices of French bread for dipping.

RUMAKI

This is also a terrific dish for brunch.

Preheat oven to 350°

¼ lb. bacon
½ can of water chestnuts
½ lb. of chicken livers, uncooked
½ cup soy sauce
¼ cup brown sugar

Cut the bacon in half. Wrap a bacon slice around a piece of water chestnut and a piece of chicken liver. Fasten with a toothpick.

Marinate the wrapped liver in a sauce of brown sugar and soy sauce for several hours.

Place in a baking dish and bake for 30 minutes. Drain the grease while baking (you could also place a roasting rack in the pan and place the rumaki on that). Pop under the broiler for a minute or two to crisp the bacon before serving.

Remove from broiler and drain thoughly. Serve hot.

Note: These can be made ahead of time and popped in the broiler just before serving.

Wine Suggestion:
German Riesling Spatlese

ESCARGOT in garlic butter

Preheat oven to 450°

1 can of 24 small or 12 large escargot (snails)
12 escargot shells
1 stick butter
1 tsp. chopped onion
2 cloves garlic, finely chopped
½ tsp. salt
twist of fresh black pepper

Cream the butter and add onion, garlic, salt and pepper.

Place the snail(s) (one large or 2 small) in the shell. Pack the remaining space in the shell with the butter mixture.

If shells are not available, place some butter and a snail in each indentation of an escargot dish.*

Place each shell in an indentation of an escargot dish and bake at 450° for 10 minutes until the butter sizzles. Serve immediately.

To eat, hold the shell with an escargot clamp and remove the snail with a small tined fork.

For a variation, try heating the snails in white wine seasoned with onion before placing them in the shells.

* An escargot pan is a circular, metal dish with indentations for the snail and shell (similar to a deviled egg dish). The snails are baked and served in the pan. Many gourmet shops sell these in sets with an escargot clamp and forks.

Wine Suggestion:
California Chardonnay or French White Burgundy

CHICKEN LIVER PATE with CURRY

1 lb. chicken livers, washed and drained
1 stick butter
2 medium onions, chopped
1 tsp. paprika
1 tsp. curry powder
1 tsp. salt
½ tsp. pepper
½ stick of softened butter

Melt a stick of butter in a large frying pan. Add the livers, onions, paprika, curry powder, salt and pepper. Cook until the livers are barely pink inside when cut, stirring frequently.

Remove from heat and drain off approximately ½ cup of the liquid (otherwise the pate will be too "soupy").

Cream ½ stick of butter (works well in a food processor). Add the liver mixture and blend until very smooth (if a food processor is used, process about 10 seconds). Mixture will be very thin.

Pour into a crock or onion soup casserole. Refrigerate overnight. When chilled, the pate will be the perfect consistency for spreading.

Serve with cocktail rye or pumpernickel and small sweet pickles.

Wine Suggestion:
A Rhone Wine

AVOCADO BOATS

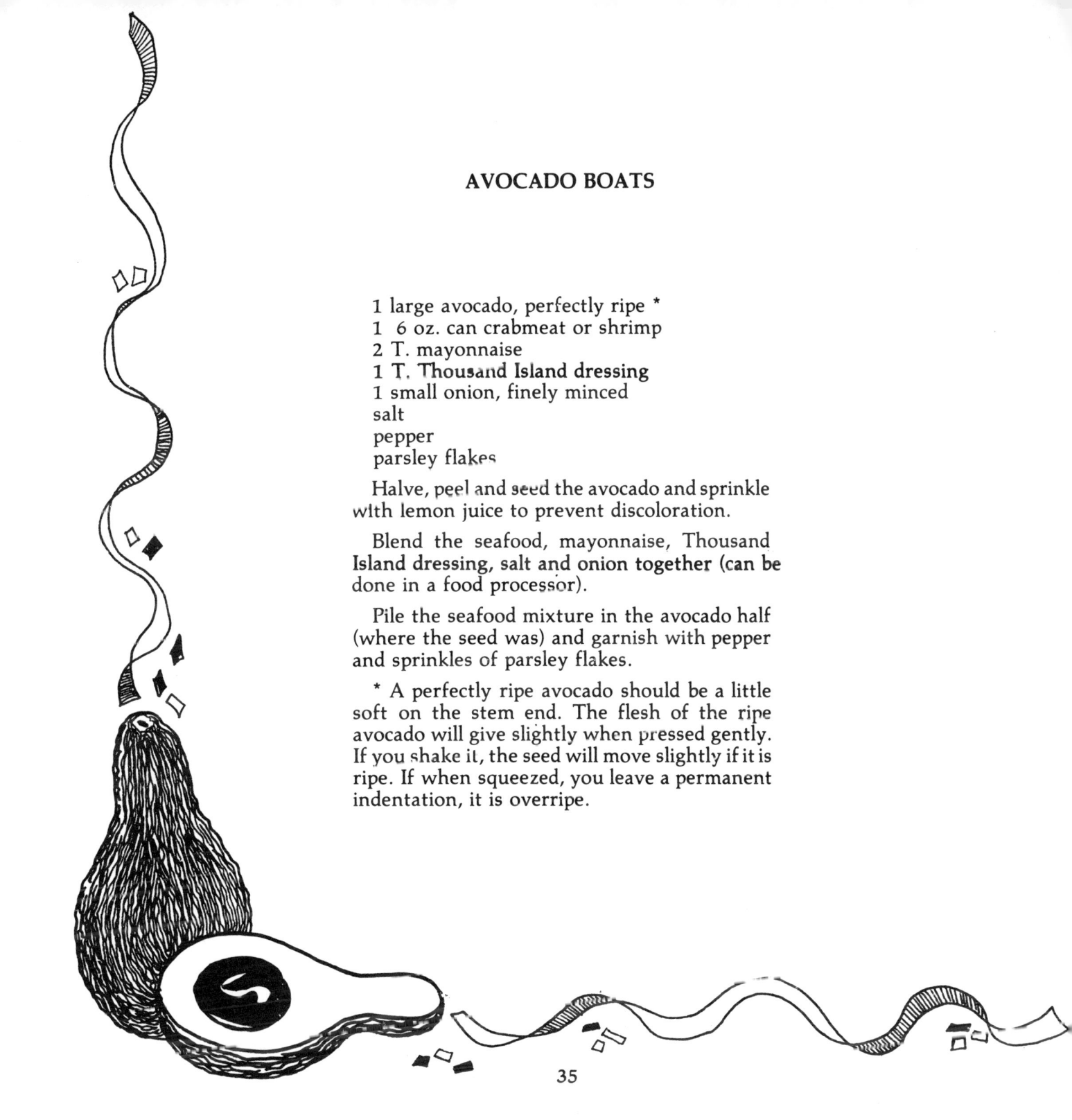

1 large avocado, perfectly ripe *
1 6 oz. can crabmeat or shrimp
2 T. mayonnaise
1 T. Thousand Island dressing
1 small onion, finely minced
salt
pepper
parsley flakes

Halve, peel and seed the avocado and sprinkle with lemon juice to prevent discoloration.

Blend the seafood, mayonnaise, Thousand Island dressing, salt and onion together (can be done in a food processor).

Pile the seafood mixture in the avocado half (where the seed was) and garnish with pepper and sprinkles of parsley flakes.

* A perfectly ripe avocado should be a little soft on the stem end. The flesh of the ripe avocado will give slightly when pressed gently. If you shake it, the seed will move slightly if it is ripe. If when squeezed, you leave a permanent indentation, it is overripe.

RED CLAM SAUCE WITH PASTA SHELLS

    2 T. olive oil
    1½ cups seasoned tomato sauce
    1 T. basil
    1/3 cup red cooking wine
    ½ tsp. salt
    ½ tsp. pepper
    ½ tsp. oregano
    1 10 oz. can baby chowder clams
    3 cups cooked pasta shells (medium size)

Heat olive oil in saucepan. Add the tomato sauce, spices and wine. Stir until well blended and simmer for 10 minutes. Add the drained clams and simmer for 3 more minutes.

Remove from heat and pour over pasta shells. Serve in ramekins or on a small plate. Sprinkle grated parmesan cheese over the top of each serving.

HOMEMADE TOMATO SAUCE

    1½ T. olive oil
    1 cup chopped onions
    3½ cups canned Italian-style plum tomatoes (drained)
    1 8 oz. can tomato sauce
    ¼ tsp. garlic salt
    ¼ tsp. freshly ground black pepper
    ½ tsp. salt
    ½ tsp. sugar
    1 bay leaf
    ½ tsp. oregano

Saute onions in olive oil over medium heat until transparent. Add remaining ingredients (except oregano), stirring well. Simmer uncovered for 45 minutes, stirring occasionally. Add oregano and continue cooking for 15 minutes. Remove bay leaf. Sauce is now ready.

Wine Suggestion:
Italian Red

海
· sea ·

SHANGHAI SHRIMP

1 10 oz. package frozen "Japanese style" vegetables
2 cans shrimp or one 6 oz. bag frozen shrimp, thawed
3 T. butter
1 tsp. white cooking wine
½ tsp. teriyaki sauce
2 T. slivered almonds
2 cups cooked rice

Cook vegetables according to package directions.

Saute shrimp in the butter for approximately 2 minutes, until cooked. Combine the shrimp and vegetables.

Add the teriyaki sauce and wine to the shrimp and vegetables and heat for 2 minutes (just to get the entire mixture heated thoroughly).

Serve over a bed of rice and top with slivered almonds.

Wine Suggestion:
German Gewurztraminer

她 · she ·   愛 · love ·   他 · he ·

STUFFED BAKED POTATOES

Preheat oven to 375°

You will need:

2 baked potatoes (perhaps dinner's leftovers)
Seafood or ham filling

Cut a cross in the top of the potato and open (just as you would if you were going to serve it with butter and sour cream). Place in an au gratin dish and pour either filling inside the potato (it's okay to overflow!). Bake at 375° for 10 minutes.

Seafood

1/3 cup chopped onion
½ stick butter
4 T. flour
2 cups milk
4 T. sherry
1 6 oz. can
   baby shrimp

Melt the butter in a saucepan and saute the onion until soft. Stir in flour and cook until golden. Slowly add the milk, stirring constantly. Cook until the sauce is smooth and thick. Stir in sherry and shrimp, Heat to serving temperature. Pour over potato, and sprinkle with parmesan cheese if desired. Bake.

AuGratin with Ham

3 T. butter
3 T. flour
1½ cups milk
1 cup grated cheddar cheese
½ tsp. salt
dash of white pepper
1/8 tsp. dry mustard
1 cup diced ham
paprika

Melt the butter in a saucepan and add the flour. Stir until blended. Add the milk gradually, stirring constantly. When sauce has thickened, add the cheese and stir until melted. Add the ham, blend and heat. Pour in potato and garnish with a few shakes of paprika.

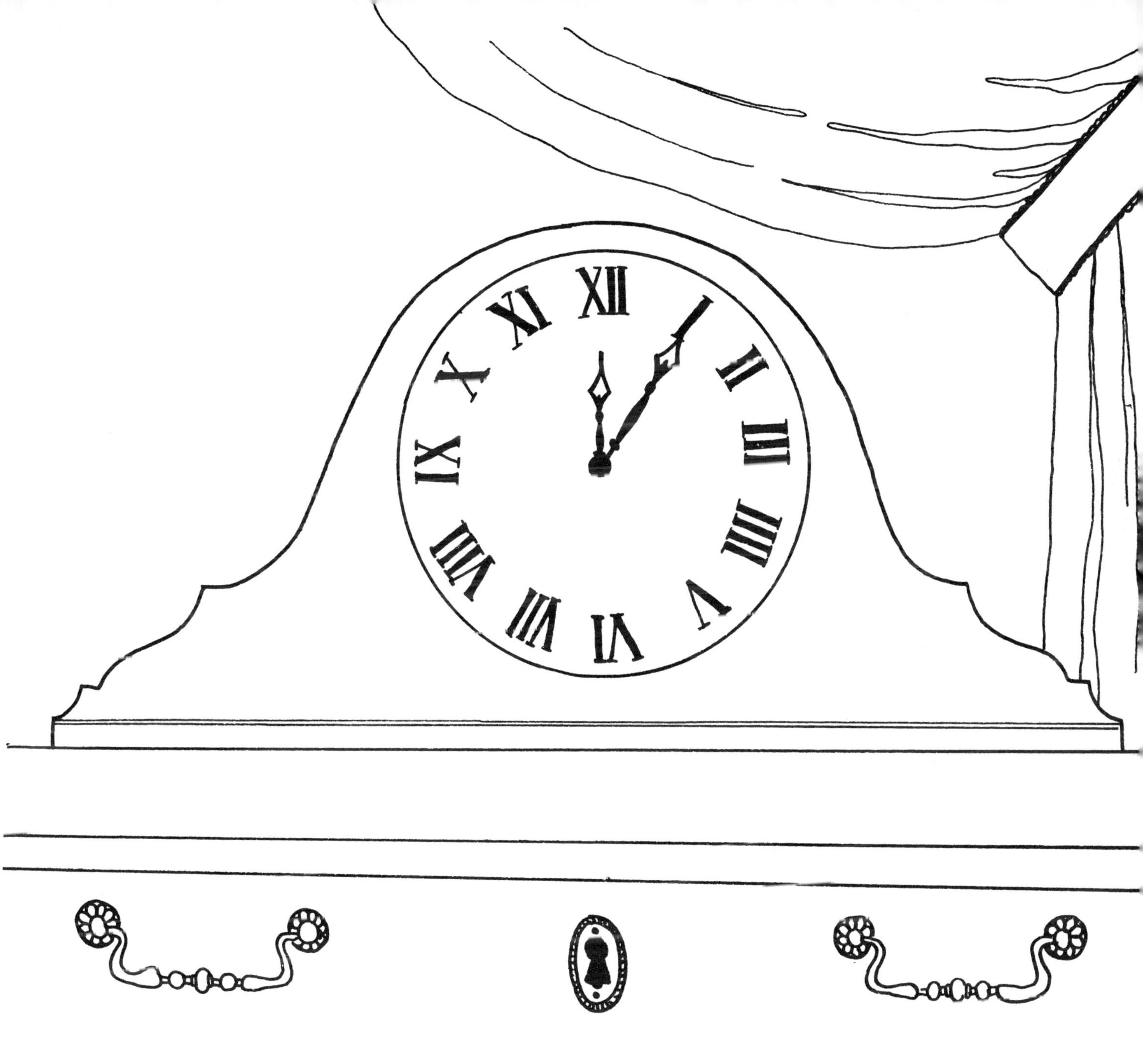

AFTER THE BALL IS OVER

Avoid the after theatre crowd at the local bistro and invite your group back to your home for an intimate get-together.

A mug of minestrone will warm your guests on a brisk night (or after an evening tobagganing).

Serve a midnight buffet of almond mushrooms, shrimp dip cocktail meatballs and olive cheese rounds, or simply offer a melange of "Finger Foods" for guests to enjoy.

Sound good? Read on and plan your next midnight culinary feast for your friends.

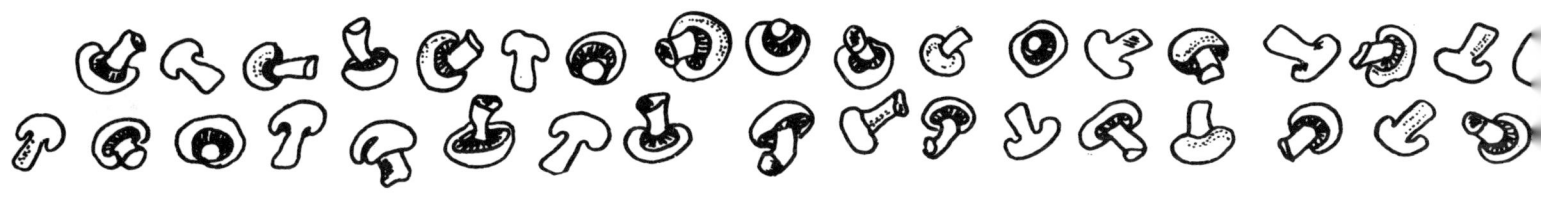

ALMOND MUSHROOMS

Preheat oven to 350°

½ lb. fresh mushrooms
½ cup bread crumbs
2 tsp. lemon juice
¼ tsp. rosemary
1/8 tsp. marjoram
¼ tsp. salt
1/3 cup chopped almonds
3 T. butter
1 T. sherry

Wash mushrooms and remove stems. Chop stems very fine and mix them with bread crumbs, lemon juice, spices, almonds, butter and sherry. Stuff the mushroom caps with the mixture and place in a glass baking dish (stuffed side up). Bake about 15 minutes and serve.

SPINACH STUFFED MUSHROOMS

Preheat oven to 350°

1 lb. fresh mushrooms, washed
½ cup chopped green onions
3 T. butter
1 10 oz. pkg. frozen, chopped spinach, thawed and squeezed dry
½ cup finely chopped Canadian bacon
1 cup cream of mushroom soup
salt
2 T. butter

Remove stems from mushrooms. Saute the green onions in the butter until transparent. Add the spinach and cook for 3 to 4 minutes. Remove from heat. Stir in the Canadian bacon and cream of mushroom soup. Place mushroom caps in a buttered glass baking dish, salt them lightly, and fill with the spinach stuffing. Bake for 10 to 12 minutes - until mushrooms are cooked. Serve on a platter.

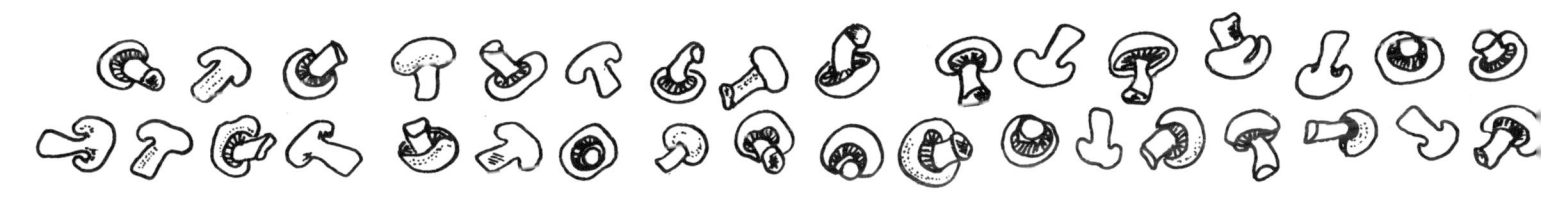

PICKLED FANCY

Marinate any or all of the following in a jar of clear Italian salad dressing (or make your own).

    julienned carrot strips
    button mushrooms
    cooked brussel sprouts
    raw cauliflower
    cocktail onions
    cooked green beans
    cucumber slices
    wedges of tomatoes
    rounds of zucchini

Serve right from the jar as a midnight snack or arrange on a tray with the following for a quick antipasto:

    provolone cheese (arrange in triangular shapes)
    prosciutto (roll the slices)
    salami
    black olives
    anchovies

Garnish the tray with slices of hard boiled eggs and serve with a crock filled with bread sticks.

DILL

AUNT GEN'S SHRIMP DIP

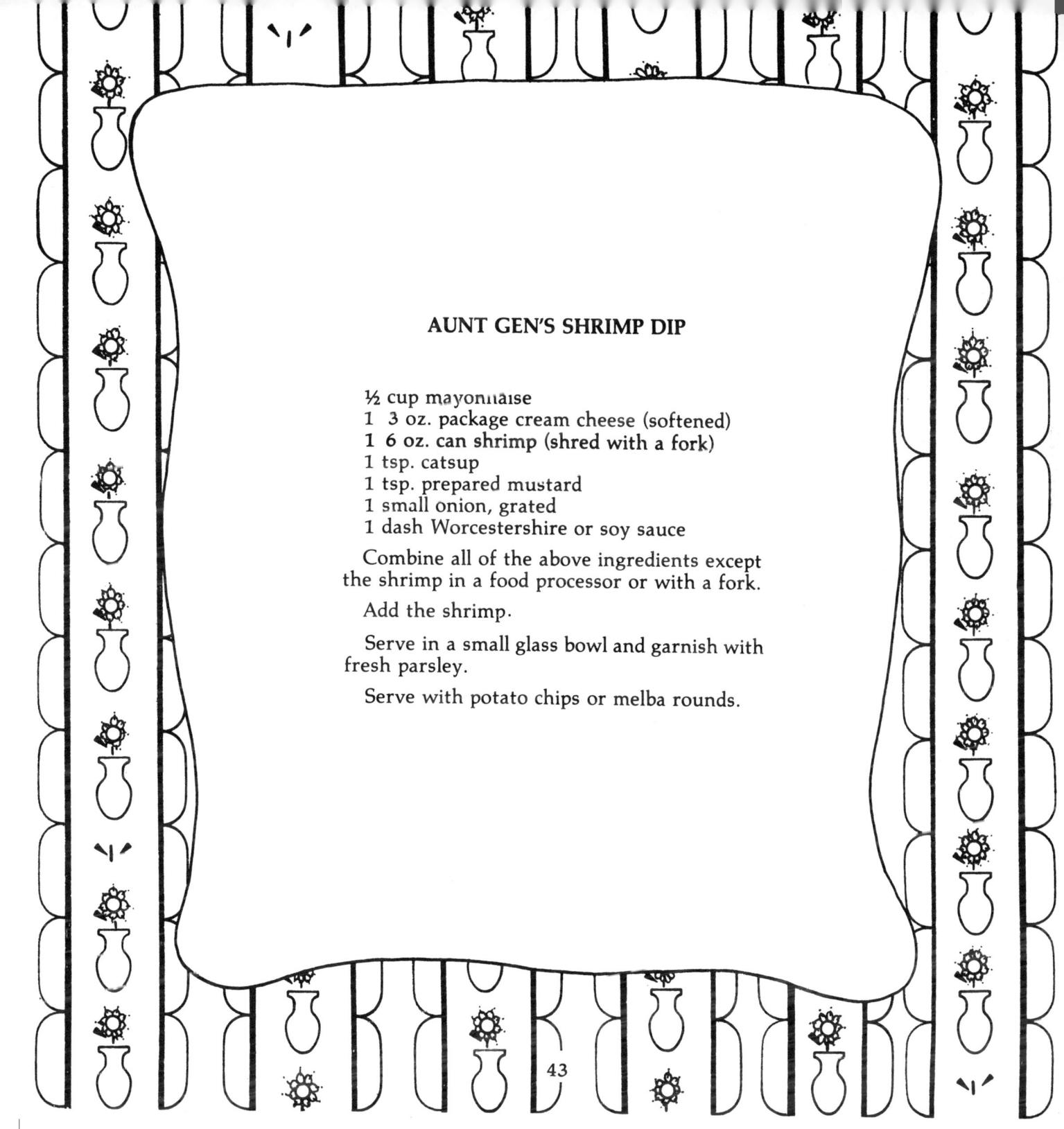

½ cup mayonnaise
1   3 oz. package cream cheese (softened)
1   6 oz. can shrimp (shred with a fork)
1 tsp. catsup
1 tsp. prepared mustard
1 small onion, grated
1 dash Worcestershire or soy sauce

Combine all of the above ingredients except the shrimp in a food processor or with a fork.

Add the shrimp.

Serve in a small glass bowl and garnish with fresh parsley.

Serve with potato chips or melba rounds.

STUFFED CHERRY TOMATOES

3 dozen cherry tomatoes (cut off the tops and scoop out most of the pulp)

Filling
In a food processor or blender combine:
1 medium avocado, halved, seeded and peeled
4 oz. cottage cheese
1 tsp. lemon juice
¼ tsp. salt
½ tsp. dried dill
2 T. grated onion

Process until smooth and fill the tomatoes. Serve chilled.

STUFFED CUCUMBERS

2 cucumbers, peeled and then rubbed with ½ tsp. salt (to extract the water)

Filling
¼ lb. slice of ham, diced
2 hard boiled eggs, chopped
2 tsp. green onions, sliced
2 T. mayonnaise or Thousand Island dressing

Cut off the tip of the cucumber (½ inch) and cut out the seeds and center pulp with a long handled spoon, leaving a ¼ inch shell.

Mix the filling ingredients until smooth. Stand the cucumber on end and stuff with the filling, packing tightly. Wrap in plastic wrap and refrigerate 2 hours. Remove from refrigerator, unwrap, and slice in ½ to 3/4 inch slices. Arrange slices on a bed of lettuce and serve immediately.

(You could also use the cream puff fillings given on p. 45)

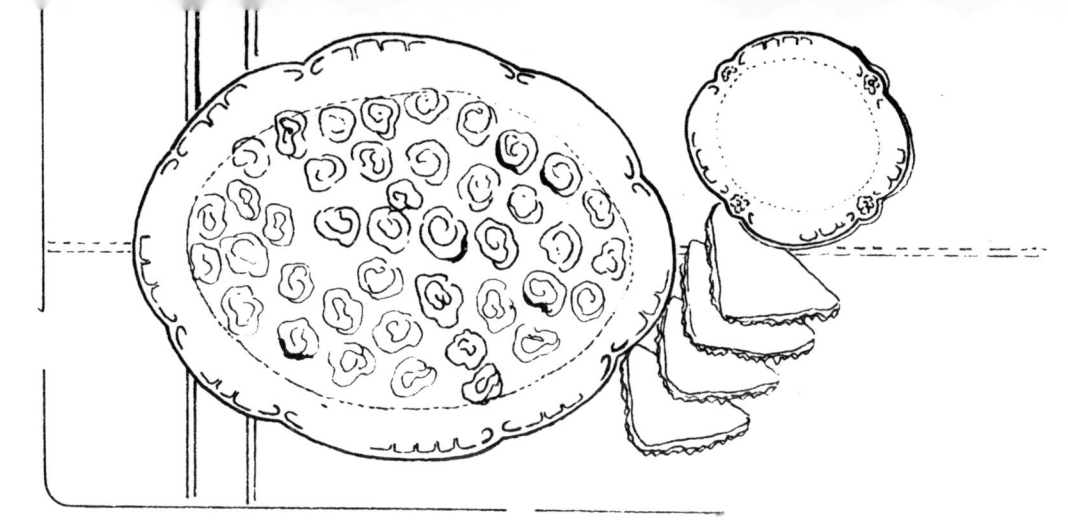

COCKTAIL CREAM PUFFS

Preheat oven to 425°

3/4 cup water
6 T. butter
3/4 cup flour
3 eggs.

Bring water and butter to a boil. Reduce heat and add flour all at once. Stir until thick and mixture forms a shiny ball (about 1 minute). Remove from heat.

Add eggs, one at a time, beating well after each addition. Mixture should be satiny and paste-like. Drop by teaspoonfuls, about 1 inch apart on a baking sheet or baking stone. Bake at 425° for 30 minutes or until done (Do not open oven while baking).

Makes 2½ to 3 dozen puffs.

FILLINGS

Deviled cheese
1 cup shredded cheddar cheese
¼ tsp. dry mustard
3 T. mayonnaise
1 tsp. grated onion
3-4 drops Tabasco sauce (optional)
½ tsp. celery seed

Mix together. Split puffs and fill with about 2 tsp. filling. Replace top of puff.

Ham
1 2½ oz. can deviled ham
1 3 oz. pkg. cream cheese
2 T. milk
1 tsp. grated onion
¼ tsp. horseradish
salt to taste

Mix ingredients. Split puffs and fill with 1 T. filling. Replace tops and serve.

Chicken
1 can boned chicken
¼ cup finely chopped celery
2 green onions, finely chopped
½ tsp. ginger
¼ cup mayonnaise
2 T. slivered almonds

Mix ingredients. Split puffs and fill. Replace tops and serve.

Anchovy
4 T. anchovy paste
1 cup cheddar cheese, grated
2 T. chili sauce

Combine ingredients and blend until smooth. Fill puffs, replace tops and bake at 425° just until cheese melts.

Note: Check sandwich fillings in chapter 1 for more ideas.

OLIVE CHEESE ROUNDS

Preheat oven to 350°

24 slices cocktail rye bread
3 T. butter
1½ cups shredded cheddar cheese
3/4 cup chopped green olives with pimentos
4 to 6 green onions chopped (including tops)
1/3 cup mayonnaise

Place bread slices on baking sheet and toast lightly on one side. Remove from oven and butter the other side of the bread.

Mix cheese, olives, onions and mayonnaise. Spread mixture evenly on bread. Bake for 5 to 8 minutes at 350° until cheese is lightly browned.

Serve while hot.

MUSHROOM TURNOVERS

Preheat oven to 350°

Cream Cheese Pastry

1/2 cup soft butter
3 oz. cream cheese
1½ cups all purpose flour
½ tsp. salt

Cream butter and cream cheese. Add flour and salt and mix until dough is stiff. Refrigerate 30 minutes before rolling and cutting 3 inch circles.

Filling

1/4 lb. fresh mushrooms, finely chopped
2 T. butter
1 T. flour
1 T. sherry
½ cup finely chopped onion
½ tsp. salt
½ tsp. pepper
¼ cup sour cream

Saute mushrooms and onion in butter in a skillet over medium heat until juices have evaporated. Sprinkle mushrooms with flour. Stir to mix well. Stir in sherry, salt and pepper. Cook, stirring constantly until mixture is almost dry (about 2 minutes). Stir in sour cream. Cool.

Place 1 slightly rounded teaspoonful of filling in the center of the 3 inch circle of dough. Fold in half and press edges to seal (extremely important to seal well).

Brush tops of turnovers with 1 egg yolk mixed with 1 T. water. Place turnovers on a baking sheet or baking stone and bake until golden brown (12 to 15 minutes) at 350°. Cool on wire racks.

Makes about 16.

STEAK TARTARE

Serves 4 - 6

1 lb. excellent quality freshly ground (fine) sirloin steak
2 tsp. Dijon mustard (such as Grey Poupon)
1 medium onion, finely grated
1 tsp. Worcestershire sauce
1 tsp. salt
½ tsp. ground black pepper
½ tsp. garlic powder
½ tsp. dried dill
1 egg yolk

Mix all of the above ingredients except the egg. Refrigerate for 1 to 2 hours so flavors blend. Shape into a ball and place in the center of a silver tray surrounded by pumpernickel or cocktail rye bread. Before serving, make an indentation in the ball of sirloin and top with an egg yolk. Serve with small dishes of anchovies and capers.

Another method of making steak tartare is to shape the ground sirloin steak (with no seasonings whatsoever) into a ball. Place it on a tray and surround it with the bread and dishes of:

salt	anchovies
pepper	chopped onions
dill	parsley
capers	chives

Guests can prepare their individual servings and season as they wish.

Note: Steak Tartare is not cooked and the meat must be fresh when bought and served. The mixture is spread on cocktail breads with a spreading knife. This should be eaten as soon as possible and not left out unrefrigerated for more than a couple of hours.

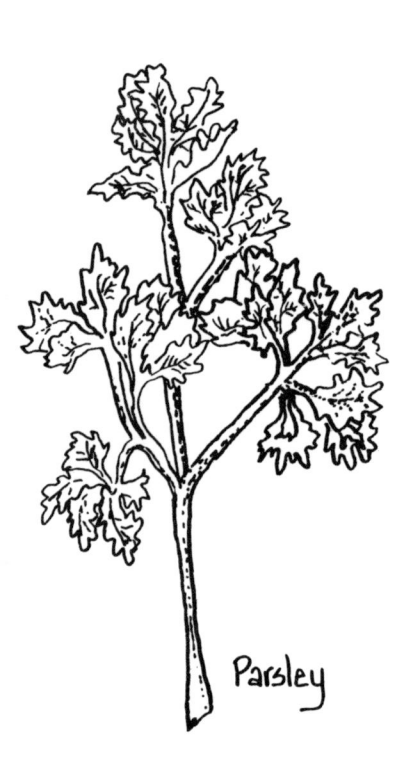

GARLIC SHRIMP FONDUE

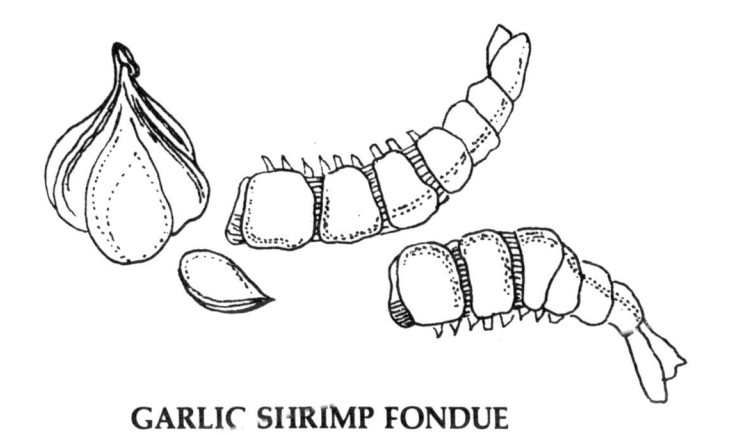

1 10 oz. can cream of shrimp soup
1 8 oz. pkg. pasteurized cheese food spread
OR
8 oz. mild cheddar cheese, shredded

4 dashes Worchestershire sauce
2 cloves garlic, finely minced
¼ lb. fresh mushrooms, sliced
2 T. butter

Wash the mushrooms. Slice and saute in butter with the garlic.

Place the soup, cheese and Worcestershire sauce in a saucepan and heat just until the cheese and soup have melted. Add the mushrooms and stir until blended. Remove from heat.

Place the mixture in a fondue pot. Serve with cubes of French bread. Spear the cube of bread on a fondue fork and dip, spearing a mushroom at the same time

BACON PECAN SPREAD

Makes about 2½ cups

8 slices bacon
1 8 oz. package cream cheese
1 cup sour cream OR cottage cheese
½ cup finely minced onion
½ cup finely minced celery
¼ cup chopped pecans
½ tsp. salt

Cook bacon until crisp. Cool, and crumble.

Mix cream cheese and sour cream OR cottage cheese in a food processor (or by hand in a mixing bowl) until very smooth. Stir in onion, celery, pecans, salt and crumbled bacon.

Mound into a cheese crock and chill. Sprinkle with bacon bits before serving, if desired. Serve with cocktail rye, bread sticks or melba rounds.

BACON PUFFS

Preheat oven to 375°

A sheet of puff pastry
4 oz. shredded cheddar cheese
2 onions, chopped
1/3 lb. bacon
1/2 cup sour cream
3 beaten eggs
½ tsp. salt
½ tsp. pepper

Sprinkle the shredded cheese over the puff pastry.

Saute the onions and bacon. Crumble the bacon. Place this over the cheese.

Blend the sour cream, eggs, salt and pepper and spoon mixture over the cheese, bacon, and onions. Bake at 375° for 30 minutes (or until the custard is set). Slice into small squares and serve.

COCKTAIL MEATBALLS

Makes 50 to 60 meatballs

2 lbs. lean ground beef
1 slightly beaten egg
1 large grated onion (it is important that it is finely grated or meatballs will not hold together when they are cooked)
½ tsp. salt.

Mix and shape the above ingredients into meatballs (use an ice cream scoop to save time or a melon baller if smaller meatballs are desired). Make sure balls are packed firmly so they do not fall apart when dropped in the sauce to cook.

Drop **uncooked** meatballs into a sauce of:

12 oz. of chili sauce
10 oz. jar grape jelly
2 T. lemon juice

Simmer meatballs in the sauce until cooked thoroughly. These can be refrigerated in the sauce for up to 2 days before serving.

To serve, bring to room temperature if they were refrigerated, heat and serve with cocktail picks from a chafing dish or fondue pot.

MINESTRONE

Will serve 8 or more

- ¼ cup olive oil
- 1 clove garlic, minced
- 1 onion, chopped
- 1 T. parsley
- ½ tsp. thyme
- 1 T. tomato paste
- 3 medium tomatoes, peeled
- 2 stalks chopped celery
- 2 diced carrots
- 2 potatoes, diced
- 1 10 oz. pkg. frozen green beans
- 6 cups water
- 6 beef boullion cubes
- 1 cup uncooked elbow macaroni
- parmesan cheese

Heat the olive oil in a large kettle. Add garlic, onions, parsley and thyme. Cook until the onion is transparent.

Add tomato paste, tomatoes, celery, carrots, potatoes, water and boullion cubes. Simmer 30 to 40 minutes.

Bring to a boil. Add the macaroni. Cook until macaroni is tender (8 - 10 minutes). Add frozen beans and simmer until the beans have cooked.

Serve in onion soup casseroles or ramekins and top with grated parmesan cheese.

SAY CHEESE...

CHEDDAR PUFFS

Preheat oven to 375°

Makes 24

1 cup water	1 cup flour
½ cup butter	4 eggs
¼ tsp. salt	¾ cup shredded sharp cheddar cheese

1 to 2 T. poppy, sesame or caraway seeds

Heat water, butter and salt in medium size saucepan until boiling. Stir in flour. Cook, stirring constantly, until mixture is smooth and almost cleans the sides of pan. Remove from heat.

Add eggs, one at a time, beating well after each addition. Beat in ½ cup of the cheese. Drop 1 T. of dough one inch apart on the baking sheet. Sprinkle each puff with remaining cheese and the seeds of your choice.

Bake until puffs are firm and golden brown (25-35 min) at 375°. Do not open oven while baking. Pierce the top of each puff with a sharp knife and bake 5 more minutes. Serve warm (or freeze tightly and reheat at 350° for 8 minutes)

CHEESE TOPPED BRUSSELS SPROUTS

Makes 24

24 medium Brussels sprouts
3 oz. cream cheese
2 T. minced onion
1 T. milk
½ tsp. dried dill

Cook brussels sprouts until crisp and tender. Rinse and cool thoroughly.

Beat cream cheese with onion, milk and dill until smooth.

Cut the bottom off of each sprout so they stand up easily. Spread the tops with the cheese mixture, mounding them up in the center. Garnish with several parsley flakes.

Refrigerate before serving.

CIDER CHEESE CROCK

4 cups grated sharp cheddar cheese
3 oz. cream cheese
½ cup apple cider or juice
2 tsp. caraway seeds (optional)
1 tsp. Worcestershire sauce
¼ tsp. white pepper

Combine all ingredients in a mixer or food processor and process until smooth. Pack into a crock and chill.

Serve with cocktail rye and wedges of apples.

CHEDDAR BALLS

Makes 70 balls

1 stick butter, softened
2/3 cup grated sharp cheddar cheese
¼ tsp. white pepper
¼ tsp. celery salt
1 cup seasoned bread crumbs

Cream the butter and mix in the cheese, pepper and celery salt (works well if done in a food processor). Shape into small balls and roll in bread crumbs. Chill at least 1 hour before serving. Serve from a wooden tray.

ARTICHOKES PARMESANO

Preheat oven to 375°

2 5 oz. jars artichoke hearts
1 cup clear Italian dressing
5 T. parmesan cheese, grated
1½ cups Italian bread crumbs
pinch of basil

Marinate sliced artichoke hearts for two hours in Italian dressing. (Drain the liquid the artichokes were packed in and replace it with Italian dressing.)

When ready to use, place remaining ingredients (cheese, bread crumbs and basil) in a small plastic bag. Coat an artichoke heart by placing gently in the bag and shaking until it is coated. Repeat with the rest of the artichokes.

Lay artichokes on a baking sheet and bake for about 15 minutes, until coating sizzles. Serve immediately.

CHICKEN DIVAN CREPES

For 12 crepes:

2 10 oz. pkg. frozen broccoli, cooked
2 cups chicken, cooked
6 T. butter
6 T. flour
2 cups chicken broth
½ cup heavy cream
1 cup parmesan cheese
4 tsp. Dijon mustard
2 T. minced onion
2 T. sherry
¼ tsp. marjoram
12 crepes (recipe for crepes is on p. 72)

Chicken filling

In a saucepan melt the butter. Blend in the flour and add the chicken broth, stirring constantly. When thickened add the cream, parmesan cheese, mustard, onion, sherry and marjoram. Stir until parmesan cheese melts.

Place a piece of broccoili in each crepe with some of the filling. Fold up each side and spoon 2 T. of filling over that. Garnish with a sprig of fresh parsley.

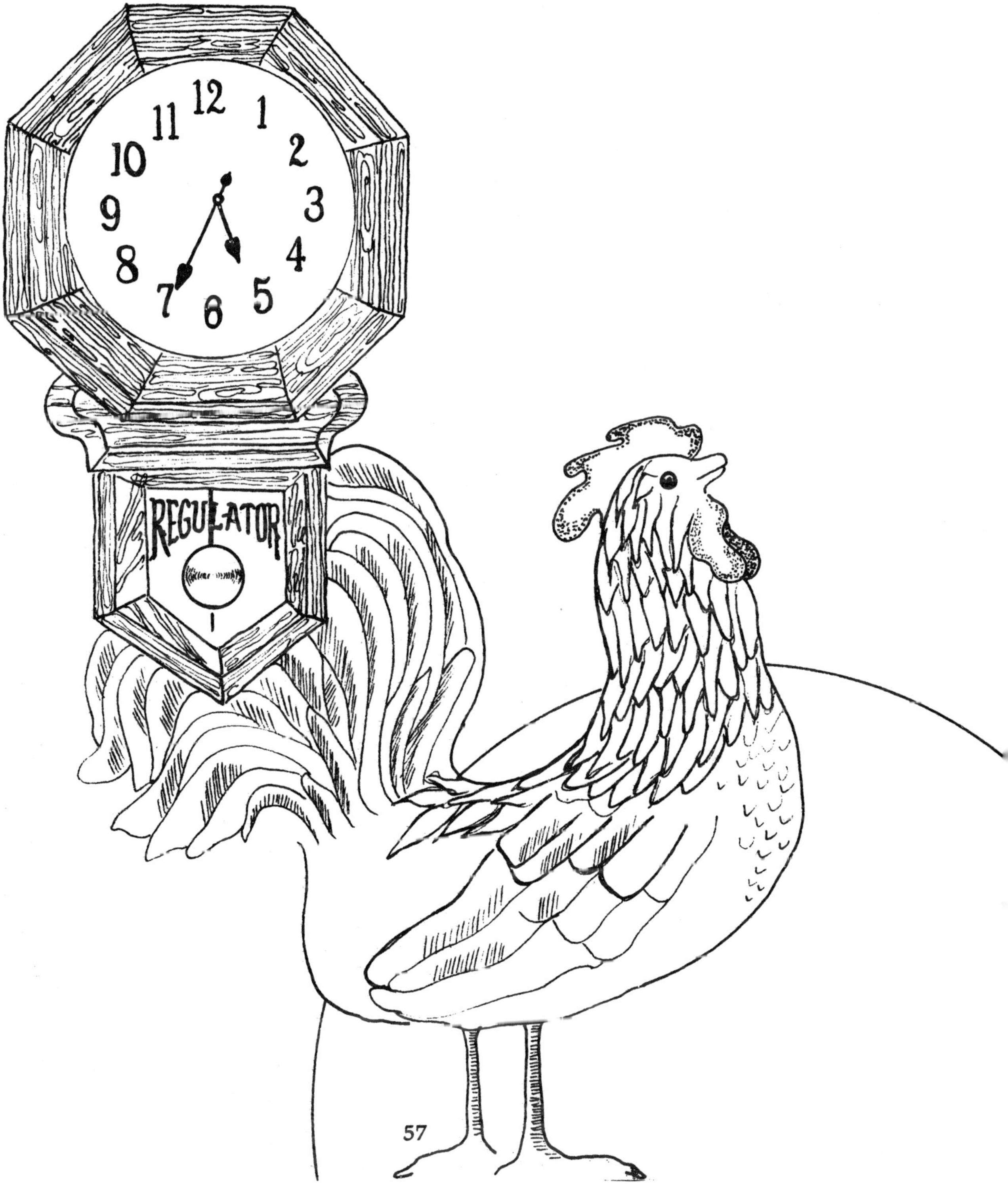
12
1
2
3
4
5
6
7
8
9
10
11
REGULATOR

THE SUN ALSO RISES

Breakfast can be more than just "a bowl of 'Cherry O's'." With a little imagination, breakfast can be as much of a culinary experience as last night's dinner.

We've given you the simplest of recipes to whip up at 3 a.m., as well as a few dishes to have on hand for the crowd that lingers on into the wee hours.

Any of these can make the morning after even more special!

(Don't forget the morning paper!)

CINNAMON FRENCH TOAST

For 2 servings

6 slices white or French bread
4 eggs
½ cup of all purpose flour
1½ to 1¾ cups of milk
½ tsp. cinnamon (or more)
1 T. butter

Beat the eggs until lemon colored. Stir in the flour to make a paste (you may have to add more or less flour to get the right consistency). Add the milk, stirring constantly with a wire whisk. Add the cinnamon.

Dip both sides of the bread in the batter and fry in a skillet, 3 slices at a time (fry in 1 T. butter). Brown one side, turn and brown the other side.

Serve using any of the toppings on p. 63 - waffle toppings.

HUEVOS RANCHEROS (Eggs, Ranch Style)

This will spark a bit of nostaligia in those who have visited Mexico!

For each serving you will need:

2 eggs
1 T. butter
1 hot, fried tortilla (Fry 1 minute per side in a lightly oiled skillet)
3 T. refried beans, canned bean dip, or canned refried beans
Salsa Picante

Spread the beans on a hot tortilla.

Melt the butter. When foam subsides, fry the two eggs. When cooked as desired, remove from heat and place the two eggs on the bean covered tortilla. Smother in Salsa Picante and serve.

Refried Beans
1 16 oz. can pinto beans
3 cloves garlic, finely minced
dash of cumin
salt and pepper to taste

Mash the beans with a fork and mix in garlic and spices. (Be very careful if you use a food processor as the beans can quickly become pureed.)

Heat 2 T. oil in a frying pan and fry the mashed bean mixture until slightly brown.

Store in a tightly covered container. If mixture becomes dry, add a little water or oil to moisten.

Salsa Picante
2 cups tomatoes, peeled and chopped
5 T. vinegar
1 cup chopped onions
2 T. green chilis (canned)
4 T. tomato paste

Combine all ingredients in a saucepan and heat until thick.
Simmer about 15 min.

ITALIAN OMELETTE

For 1 serving

3 eggs
salt
pepper
1 tomato, peeled, chopped and drained
¼ tsp. oregano
½ tsp. basil
¼ cup mozzarella cheese

Beat eggs with a wire whisk until well blended. Add a pinch of salt and a twist of pepper. Heat an omelette pan, add a pat of butter to one half (the side opposite the handle) and pour in the egg mixture to the buttered half. Stir continuously without disturbing the bottom crust. Add the tomatoes, oregano, basil and cheese to the eggs.

Fold the "unfilled" half over and close the omelette pan. Finish cooking until the eggs are set.

Serve with a sprig of fresh parsley.

PANCAKES ala ORANGE

Makes 10-12 pancakes

1 beaten egg
1 cup light cream
1 6 oz. can frozen orange juice concentrate
1 cup pancake mix

Combine the egg, cream and one-fourth of the orange juice concentrate. (Set aside the remainder of the concentrate for the orange syrup). Add the pancake mix and stir with a wire whisk until smooth.

Fry pancakes on a lightly greased griddle, flipping when lightly browned. Serve with heated orange syrup, a slice of orange and a flaming sugar cube*.

ORANGE SYRUP

1 stick butter
1 cup sugar
Remaining can of frozen orange
  juice concentrate
1 T. Grand Marnier (optional)

Heat the above ingredients (except the liqueur) to boiling, stirring occasionally. Heat until the mixture thickens and the sugar is dissolved. Remove from heat and add the Grand Marnier.

*For flaming sugar cube, soak a sugar cube in lemon or orange extract and light.

PECAN WAFFLES

Preheat waffle iron

Truly worth the trouble to make them from scratch.

Serves 4, generously

2 cups sifted all purpose flour
3 tsp. baking powder
2 T. sugar
1 tsp. salt
3 eggs, separated
1¼ cups milk
4 T. vegetable oil
2/3 cup chopped pecans

Sift dry ingredients (flour, baking powder, sugar and salt). Beat egg yolks and add to the milk and oil. Combine the dry ingredients with the egg yolk/milk/oil mixture, blending thoroughly.

Beat egg whites until stiff. Fold the egg whites and pecans into the batter (don't skimp on the pecans!).

Make the waffles as you would regular waffles, using a heated waffle iron.

Serve hot with any of the following toppings.

WAFFLE TOPPINGS

- powdered sugar and cinnamon
- heated maple syrup with chopped pecans
- warmed fruit in natural syrup
- heated applesauce
- spiced whipped cream (flavored with cinnamon and nutmeg)
- equal parts of honey and sour cream beaten until fluffy
- 1 tsp. molasses, a twist of lemon and pat of butter

PANCAKE NONPAREIL

Preheat oven to 425°

Serves 4-6

½ cup flour
½ cup milk
2 eggs
a pinch of nutmeg
4 T. butter
2 T. confectioners sugar
Juice of ½ lemon

In a mixing bowl, combine the flour, milk, eggs and nutmeg. Beat lightly. (leave the batter a little lumpy).

Melt butter in a 12" skillet with heatproof handle. When very hot, pour in the batter. Bake in oven 15 to 20 minutes or until golden brown.

Sprinkle with sugar and return briefly to oven. Sprinkle with lemon juice, then serve with jelly, jam or marmalade.

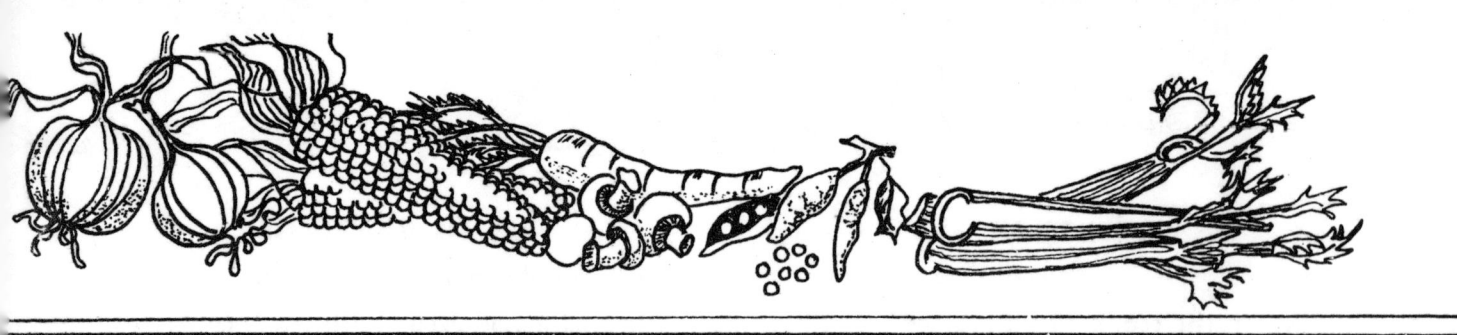

GARDEN QUICHE

Preheat oven to 400°

1 9" pie shell (either frozen or homemade)
1 10 oz. pkg. frozen mixed vegetables
¼ cup chopped onion
2 cups shredded Swiss cheese
4 eggs
1¼ cups light cream
1 tsp. salt
¼ tsp. white pepper
¼ tsp. thyme

Cook the vegetables and the onion together, using the directions on the package of vegetables. Set aside.

Bake the pie shell at 400° for 6 to 8 minutes. Remove from oven and brush with a beaten egg. Return to oven and bake one more minute.

For filling, beat 3 remaining eggs and the cream until light and fluffy (best if you use a wire whisk). Blend in salt, pepper and thyme.

Sprinkle the cheese on the pie shell, and top with the vegetable/onion mixture. Pour the filling over this mixture and dot with butter.

Bake at 400° for 35 minutes, until a knife inserted in the center comes out clean, top is brown, and custard does not "jiggle". (Do not open oven while quiche is rising). Serve immediately.

PATE BRISEE (pie crust)

6 T. chilled butter
2 T. lard
3-5 T. ice water
1½ cups all-purpose flour
¼ tsp. salt

Combine butter, lard, flour and salt. Blend until flour has the appearance of course meal. Sprinkle the ice water over the mixture, toss lightly and gather the dough into a ball. If dough seems crumbly, add more water. Cover with plastic wrap and refrigerate for an hour. Roll out dough to fit a 9" pie plate. Prick the bottom of the shell all over with a fork before baking as above.

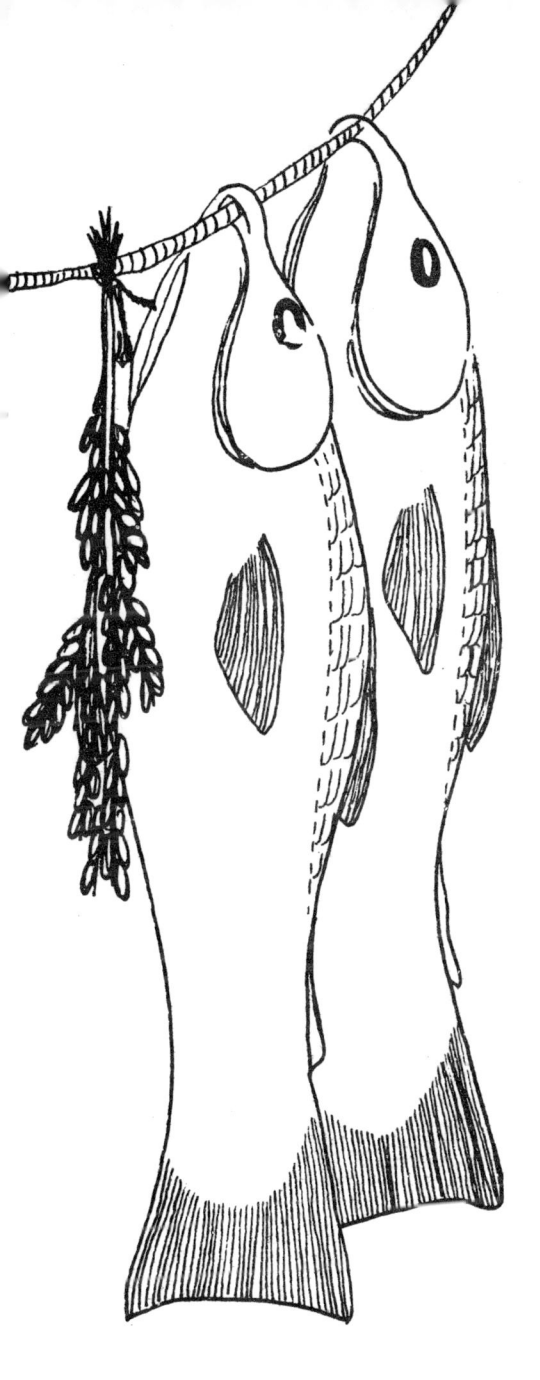

SALMON MOUSSE WITH DILL SAUCE

3 T. flour	½ cup herbed vinegar
3 T. confectioners sugar	(make your own or substitute tarragon vinegar)
2 tsp. Dijon mustard	
2 tsp. salt	3 T. melted butter
dash of white pepper	2 envelopes un-flavored gelatin
4 eggs	
1½ cups of milk	¼ cup cold water
	3 cups canned salmon
	1 cup whipping cream, whipped

Mix the flour, sugar, mustard, salt and white pepper in the top of a double boiler. Add the beaten eggs and blend until smooth with a wire whisk. Add the milk, stirring constantly. Stir in vinegar slowly, stirring constantly (otherwise it will sour the milk). Add the melted butter. Cook until thick, continuously stirring.

Soften the gelatin in cold water and add to the cooking mixture, again stirring constantly. Add the salmon. Chill (stir from time to time with a wooden spoon).

When mixture starts to thicken fold in the whipped cream until completely blended. Place in a 2 quart mold (preferably a fish shaped mold) and chill until firm. Serve on lettuce and a side dish of dill sauce.

DILL SAUCE

1 cucumber (peeled, seeded and shredded)
1 cup sour cream
1 T. lemon juice
1 tsp. dill
1 tsp. chives
pinch of salt
pinch of tarragon

Mix the shredded cucumber with a few shakes of salt and let it sit for about an hour (this extracts the water). Drain completely. Combine the cucumber with remaining ingredients and chill. Serve in a gravy dish with the mousse.

This sauce works beautifully when made in a food processor. Both the mousse and sauce can be made the day before.

GLAZED FRUIT SKEWERS

Place any of the following fruits on short skewers:

peeled oranges
hulled strawberries
red apples (peels left on)
dates
pineapple
melon balls
grapes

In a saucepan combine:

2 cups granulated sugar
½ cup honey
½ cup water

Bring to a boil and continue boiling until a small amount dropped in cold water forms a hard ball (300° on candy thermometer).

Dip skewers of fruit into the syrup and plunge into ice water to cool immediately. Allow to remain in ice water several seconds. Remove and place on a glass, lettuce lined platter. Serve at once.

FROSTED FRUIT COMPOTES

Dip champagne glasses in beaten egg white and then in colored granulated sugar. Let dry.

Strawberry

(Use red colored sugar)
Fill glass with fresh strawberries and cover with Marsala wine. Sprinkle with 1½ tsp. colored sugar. Garnish with a sprig of mint. Serve.

Melon

(Use green colored sugar)
Place various melon balls in glass and sprinkle with 1½ tsp. green sugar. Fill glass with apple cider. Serve.

CHINESE ORANGE ROLLS

1 package won ton skins (available in the produce section or freezer case)
1 jar orange marmalade
1 egg, lightly beaten
oil for deep frying

Place the won ton skin in front of you so the corner is facing you and appears in the shape of a diamond.

Place a teaspoonful of orange marmalade in the center of the skin. Fold the bottom end up over the marmalade. Fold each side in and roll up tightly.

Seal the end well with a beaten egg so the roll keeps its shape.

Fry in hot oil until nicely browned. Drain on paper towels and serve immediately, dusted with confectioners sugar.

SPIKED AND SPICED COFFEES

Hawaiian
For each serving:

Scald ½ cup coconut milk (canned). Pour into a coffee mug and add ½ cup strong, hot coffee. Serve.

Cinnamon
For each serving:

In a cup of hot black coffee add 1 T. heavy cream and 1 cinnamon stick. Top with a pat of butter.

Mocha Chocolate
For each serving:

Pour equal amounts of hot chocolate and strong coffee into a mug. Top with whipped cream and a twist of orange peel and serve.

Rum
For each serving:

Combine 1½ tsp. sugar and 1 T. hot coffee in a mug. Add ¼ cup warm rum and fill with hot coffee. Top with whipped cream.

Irish
For each serving:

In a mug combine 2/3 cup hot coffee 1 tsp. sugar, and 3 T. Irish whiskey Stir and top with whipped cream.

Mexican
For each serving:

In a mug combine 2/3 cup hot coffee, 2 T. Kahlua, and 1 tsp. Drambuie Top with whipped cream.

TIJUANA CHOCOLATE
For one serving:

Combine:

⅛ tsp. cinnamon
1 oz. brandy

in a mug. Fill with espresso* coffee. Top with a scoop of chocolate ice cream.

*Espresso can be bought in instant, powdered form. If you wish to use this, add ¾ cup of hot water to 1 tsp. powdered coffee.

Espresso is the best known coffee of Italy. It is approximately 4 times stronger than American coffee. True espresso is made with an expresso maker - a machine that forces hot water through a sieve under tremendous pressure. Cappucino is expresso mixed with an equal amount of milk and steamed until frothy.

COFFEE ROYAL
For one serving:

3 slices of lemon peel
½ cinnamon stick
powdered sugar
1½ oz. cognac
½ cup of hot, strong coffee

Rub one of the lemon peels around the rim of a small size mug. Dip the rim in powdered sugar. Place the lemon peels in a mug with the cinnamon stick. Warm the cognac over a low flame (you can place the cognac in a ladel and hold the ladel over the flame). Pour the warmed cognac in a mug and light. When flame burns out add the coffee. Top with whipped cream and serve.

12:03 AM

HOW SWEET IT IS

"How Sweet It Is" to dig into something fruity, gooey, nutty or chocolately. We've taken special care to select a variety of concoctions that divert from traditional cakes & cookies. "Strawberries elegante" or "Toffee torte" are great just before retiring while "Spiced nuts" or "Peanut butter balls" are a good combination for the late movie. From the very sweet "Apricot coconut balls" to the bittersweet "Mandarin orange chocolate sauce," there's something for everyone's liking.

CHERRIES JUBILEE

Using **canned** cherries

1 #2 can of large black cherries
2 T. sugar
1 T. cornstarch
½ cup cognac or brandy

Drain the cherries, reserving the liquid. Mix the cherry liquid with the sugar and cornstarch. Place in a saucepan and bring to a boil until thick. Turn off heat.

Add the cherries and liqueur and stir gently to blend.

Serve over vanilla ice cream.

Using **fresh** cherries

1 lb. black or bing cherries
¾ cup water
½ cup sugar
1 tsp. cornstarch dissolved in 1 T. water
½ cup cognac or brandy

Wash, stem and pit cherries. Cook the water and sugar until thickened. Add the cherries and simmer until the cherries are tender but not mushy. Remove the cherries and set aside. Continue cooking the syrup for about 5 minutes, stirring constantly. Add the cornstarch/water and stir until thick. Fold in the cherries and cognac gently and remove from heat.

Serve over vanilla ice cream

blintzes • apricot • suzette • raisin • mincemeat • toffee • chocolate • strawberry • vanilla • cherry • apple • ice cream • lemon • peach • pecan •

DESSERT CREPES

For 12 crepes

Crepes

1 cup flour
pinch of salt
3 eggs
1½ cups of milk
½ cup of oil for frying

Mix the flour and salt. Add the eggs, one at a time, making a paste. While stirring with a wire wisk, add the milk. Allow batter to rest in the refrigerator for 1 hour until well chilled. (Batter can be left until the next day and then thinned with 1 to 2 T. milk). For each crepe, place 1 tsp. of vegetable oil in a crepe pan. Heat and spread the oil over the entire bottom of the pan. Ladle enough crepe batter into the pan to cover the bottom (tilt pan in all directions until batter evenly covers the bottom). Place the pan back on the burner and cook for about 30 seconds, or until bubbles begin to form in the crepe. Turn crepe and cook the other side for about 30 seconds and serve.

(When frying crepes, keep the batter very cold by placing the bowl in an ice bath).

Fillings

Blueberry

2 pints blueberries, washed
½ cup red wine (not cooking wine)
½ cup orange juice
4 T. currant jelly
1 T. cornstarch

Combine jelly, wine and orange juice and bring to the boiling point in a small saucepan. Dissolve the cornstarch in 2 T. **cold** water and add to the boiling mixture. Stir just until it thickens.

Remove from heat and gently add the blueberries. Put 2 T. filling in each crepe and roll up. Place in a buttered dish, dot with butter and bake at 350° for 10 minutes. Serve warm, with a scoop of vanilla ice cream or a dollop of whipped cream.

Apple

2 lbs. cooking apples
3 T. sugar
1 T. cinnamon
2 T. butter

Peel, core and dice the apples. Melt the butter in a frying pan and add apples, sprinkling with sugar and cinnamon. Fry just until browned (but not mushy).

Place the apples in a crepe and bake for 10 minutes at 350°. Serve with spiced whipped cream (whipped cream with cinnamon and nutmeg) and toasted pecans.

Crepes are delicious when filled with any flavor of ice cream and then folded and smothered in sauce. For ideas for other fillings, see p. 22, "Ice cream toppings for one." Any of these make an excellent crepe filling.

Hot dessert crepes can also be made by filling crepes with a good quality preserve, rolling and dusting with confectioners sugar.

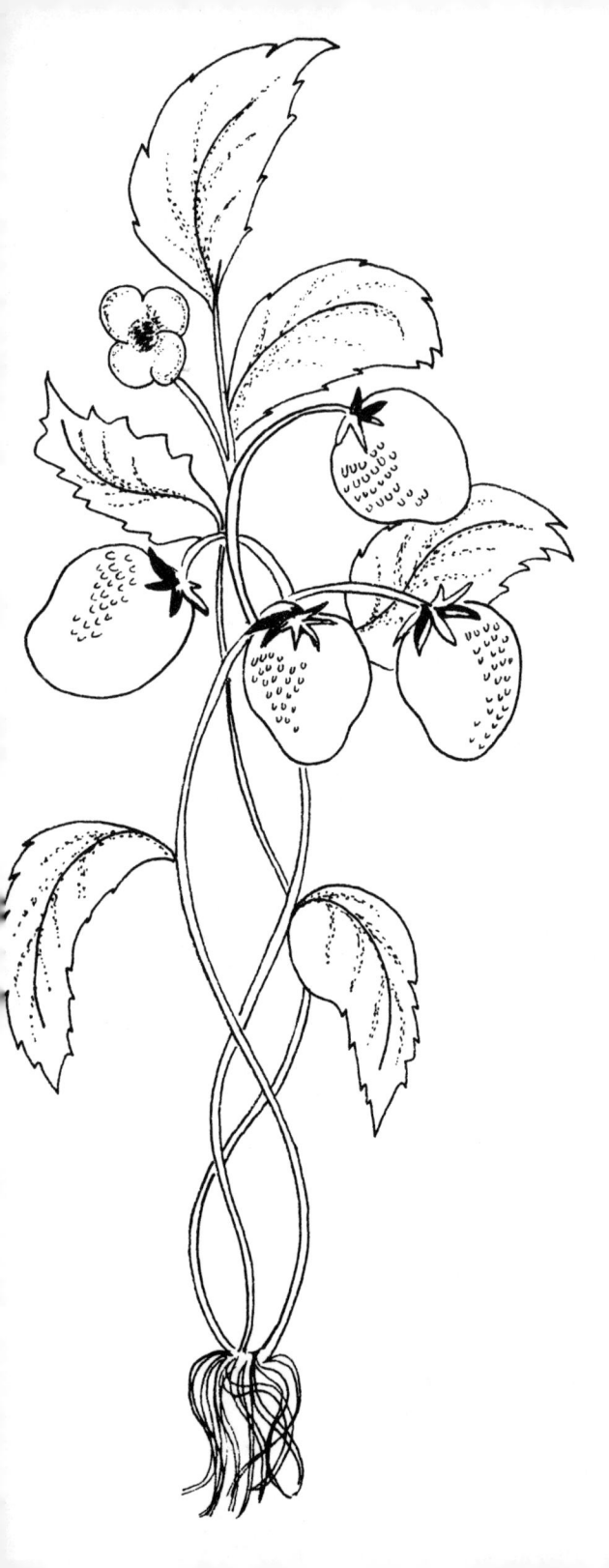

STRAWBERRIES ELEGANTE'

For each serving you will need:

1 cup sliced strawberries (fresh)
3 T. sour cream
4 T. light brown sugar

About 1 hour before serving, toss the sliced berries with 2 T. of the brown sugar. Refrigerate.

At serving time, gently fold the berries in the sour cream with the remaining brown sugar.

Serve in a frosted champagne glass, mounding the mixture in the center. Garnish with a perfect strawberry.

This is as simple and foolproof as it reads, yet tastes like it took hours to prepare.

For strawberry crepes, place the strawberry/cream mixture in a crepe, fold over both sides and place a dollop of sour cream and a fresh strawberry on the top for garnish.

EASY FUDGE

2 cups sugar
4 T. cocoa
1 5 oz. can evaporated milk
1 6 oz. pkg. semi-sweet chocolate chips
2 T. butter

Blend the sugar, cocoa and evaporated milk in a saucepan and bring to a boil.

Remove from heat and add the butter and chocolate chips. Stir with a wooden spoon until chips are well blended.

Pour into a greased 8" x 8" pan and cool. Cut into small squares and place in confectionary paper cups.

Variations:

You may wish to add any of the following when you add the chocolate chips for a variation:

- miniature marshmallows
- Spanish peanuts
- chopped walnuts
- raisins
- chopped, dried apricots
- coconut
- chopped, candied cherries
- coursely grated orange rind
- pecans
- whole almonds

CHOCOLATE DESSERT WAFFLES

4 servings   Preheat waffle iron

1 6 oz. pkg. semi-sweet chocolate chips
1/3 cup vegetable oil
1 T. baking soda
1 cup flour
¼ tsp. salt
2 eggs
½ cup sugar
½ cup milk

Melt chocolate pieces in oil in a double boiler. Set aside.

Beat the eggs until thick and lemon colored. Gradually add the sugar to the beaten eggs.

Combine the baking soda, flour and salt and add to the sugar/egg mixture alternating with the milk. Finally, stir in the chocolate mixture and blend until batter is smooth.

Proceed as you would when making regular waffles in a waffle iron.

Dust waffles with confectioners sugar and serve with coffee or vanilla ice cream and a dollop of whipped cream, or sandwich a square of vanilla ice cream (cut in a square shape) between two waffles.

HOMEMADE CHOCOLATE SAUCE

Makes 1 cup

2 squares unsweetened chocolate
5 T. milk
½ cup sugar
dash of salt
3 T. butter
¼ tsp. vanilla

Melt the chocolate and milk over very low heat. Remove from heat when chocolate is almost melted. Add the sugar and salt and return to heat. Cook until smooth, stirring constantly. Stir in butter and vanilla. Cool.

(This may be stored in a jar in the refrigerator for later use.)

MANDARIN ORANGE CHOCOLATE DESSERT SAUCE

1 6 oz. package semi-sweet chocolate chips
¾ cup light cream
2 T. grated orange rind
¼ cup orange liqueur (Triple Sec, Grand Marnier, Cointreu)

Melt the chocolate chips in a double boiler over boiling water. Add the remaining ingredients and stir until smooth. Be careful not to overheat or the chocolate will become grainy.

Remove from heat and place in a fondue pot on a tray, with any of the following:

- marshmallows
- strawberries
- grapes
- pineapple chunks
- raisins
- dates
- banana slices
- pound cake, angel food or white layer cake cubes

Using fondue skewers, dip any of these into the fondue and enjoy.

HAWAIIAN PIE

1 10 inch graham cracker crust
  (either store bought or homemade)
2 bananas, sliced
1 20 oz. can crushed pineapple,
  well drained
1 14 oz. can sweetened condensed milk
¼ cup lemon juice
1 cup whipped cream
½ cup chopped pecans
flaked coconut

Place the bananas on the bottom crust, distributing them evenly. Cover the bananas with the drained, crushed pineapple.

Beat the sweetened condensed milk with the lemon juice until smooth (a wire whisk works well). Pour this over the pineapple.

Fold the nuts into the whipped cream and spread this over the pineapple. Top the creation with flaked coconut so the top of the pie is thoroughly covered.

Chill thoroughly (best if chilled overnight so the flavors blend).

This serves 8 to 10 people, as each slice is very rich and a small serving goes a long way.

For a special occasion, try color tinting the coconut before placing on the pie.

APRICOT COCONUT BALLS

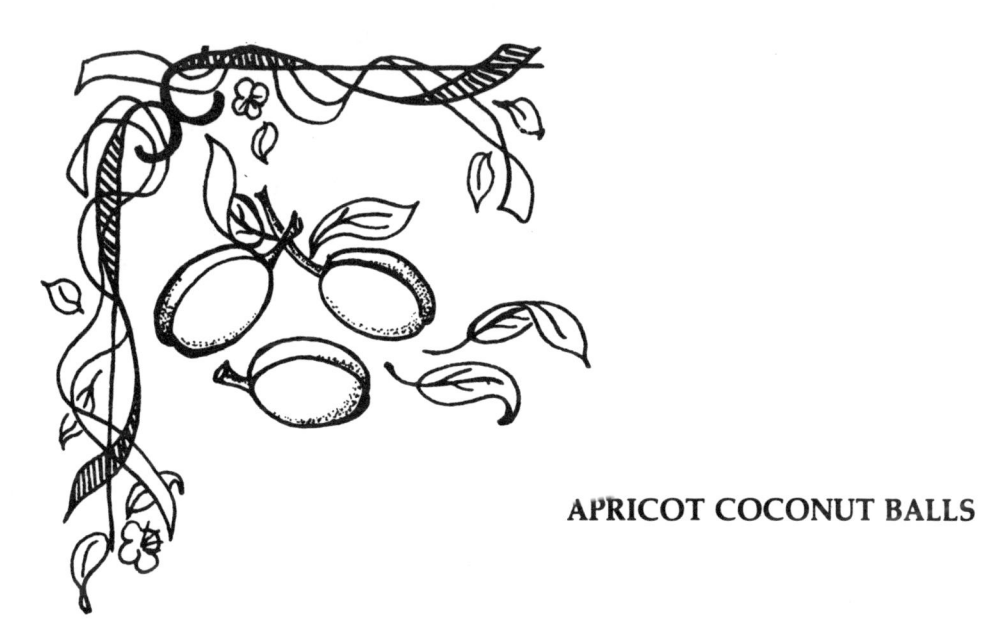

Makes 24

Combine:

¾ cup dried apricots, chopped
½ cup chopped nuts
¾ cup shredded coconut
2 T. confectioners sugar

Mix thoroughly (works very well in a food processor) and shape the mixture into small balls.

Roll the balls in chopped nuts until coated. If a sweeter candy is desired use confectioners sugar. Store in a tightly covered container.

MERINGUE NUT KISSES

Makes 48   Preheat oven to 250°

4 - 5 egg whites (depending on the size of egg used)
¼ tsp. cream of tartar
pinch of salt
1¼ cup sugar
2 tsp. vanilla
½ cup finely chopped nuts

Combine egg whites and cream of tartar. Beat the mixture until soft peaks form.* Slowly add the sugar until there are stiff peaks. Fold in the vanilla and nuts.

Line baking sheets with brown paper. Place teaspoonfuls of the meringue on the paper, evenly spaced.

Bake at 250° about 2 hours. Do not open the oven while baking.

Remove from oven, and transfer kisses from paper to a plate while still warm.

Variations:
Chocolate: Reduce vanilla to 1 tsp. and add 3 T. sifted cocoa.
Coconut: Fold in ¾ cup shredded coconut before baking
Praline: Fold in ¾ cup finely crushed peanut brittle before baking
Date: Fold in ¾ cup finely chopped dates before baking

* Egg whites beat easier if you place the mixing bowl and beaters in the freezer for about 5 minutes before beating egg whites.

TOFFEE TORTE

16 squares

2 packages ladyfingers (12 per package)
1 8 oz. carton of heavy cream, whipped
6 toffee candy bars (e.g. "Heath" brand) crushed

Line an 8" x 8" pan with 1 package of the ladyfingers.

Fold the crushed toffee candy into the whipped cream.

Spread the whipped cream over the ladyfingers in the pan.

Top with the remaining package of ladyfingers.

Freeze at least 1 hour. Then cut into squares and serve with chocolate sauce (See page 76).

RUM LOGS

4 cups vanilla wafer crumbs (1 12 oz. package of wafers, crushed)
1¼ cups chopped walnuts
1 3½ oz. can flaked coconut
1 14 oz. can sweetened condensed milk
2/3 cup rum
confectioners sugar

Combine the vanilla wafer crumbs, nuts and coconut. Stir in the sweetened condensed milk and rum. Chill the mixture until firm (4 to 6 hours).

Shape mixture into small logs or 1 tsp. balls. Roll in confectioners sugar and store in an airtight container in the refrigerator (can be stored up to a month). You may want to roll in confectioners sugar again just before serving.

Both of these recipes add a different touch to your Christmas cookie tray. Place in confectionery paper cups on a tray or in small boxes for gifts.

SPICED NUTS
Preheat oven to 225°

1 egg white
1 T. cold water
1 lb. pecan halves, unsalted
½ cup sugar
¼ tsp. salt
1 tsp. cinnamon

Beat egg white and water until frothy. Stir in pecan halves and mix until the pecans are thoroughly coated.

Blend sugar, salt and cinnamon. Add the pecan/egg-white mixture and stir until the nuts are well coated with the sugar mixture.

Spread nuts on a greased cookie sheet and bake for 1 hour. Stir every 15 minutes while the nuts are cooking so they are evenly coated with the mixture. Serve.

BRANDIED ALMONDS
Preheat oven to 350°

¼ cup butter
2¼ cups confectioners sugar
¼ cup brandy
2 cups blanched almonds

Cream the butter and blend in sugar and brandy. Set aside

Toast the almonds in a 350° oven by placing in a shallow pan and baking about 10 minutes, stirring frequently.

Remove from oven and stir in sugar mixture while nuts are hot. When nuts are well coated, spread them out on brown paper to cool, making sure to keep them separated.

Serve in crocks or small bowls as you would mixed nuts.

PEANUT BUTTER MALLOWS

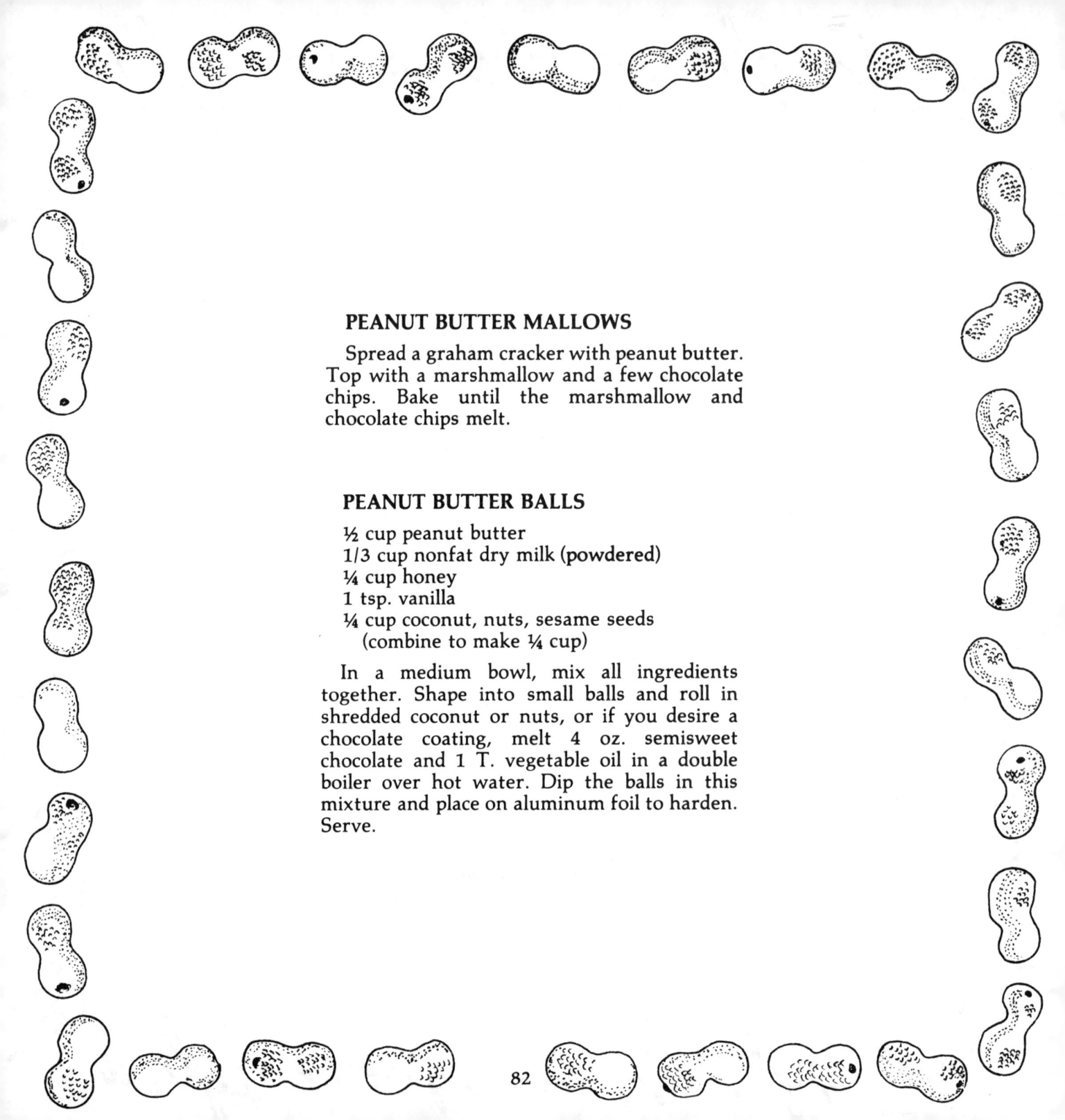

Spread a graham cracker with peanut butter. Top with a marshmallow and a few chocolate chips. Bake until the marshmallow and chocolate chips melt.

PEANUT BUTTER BALLS

½ cup peanut butter
1/3 cup nonfat dry milk (powdered)
¼ cup honey
1 tsp. vanilla
¼ cup coconut, nuts, sesame seeds
   (combine to make ¼ cup)

In a medium bowl, mix all ingredients together. Shape into small balls and roll in shredded coconut or nuts, or if you desire a chocolate coating, melt 4 oz. semisweet chocolate and 1 T. vegetable oil in a double boiler over hot water. Dip the balls in this mixture and place on aluminum foil to harden. Serve.

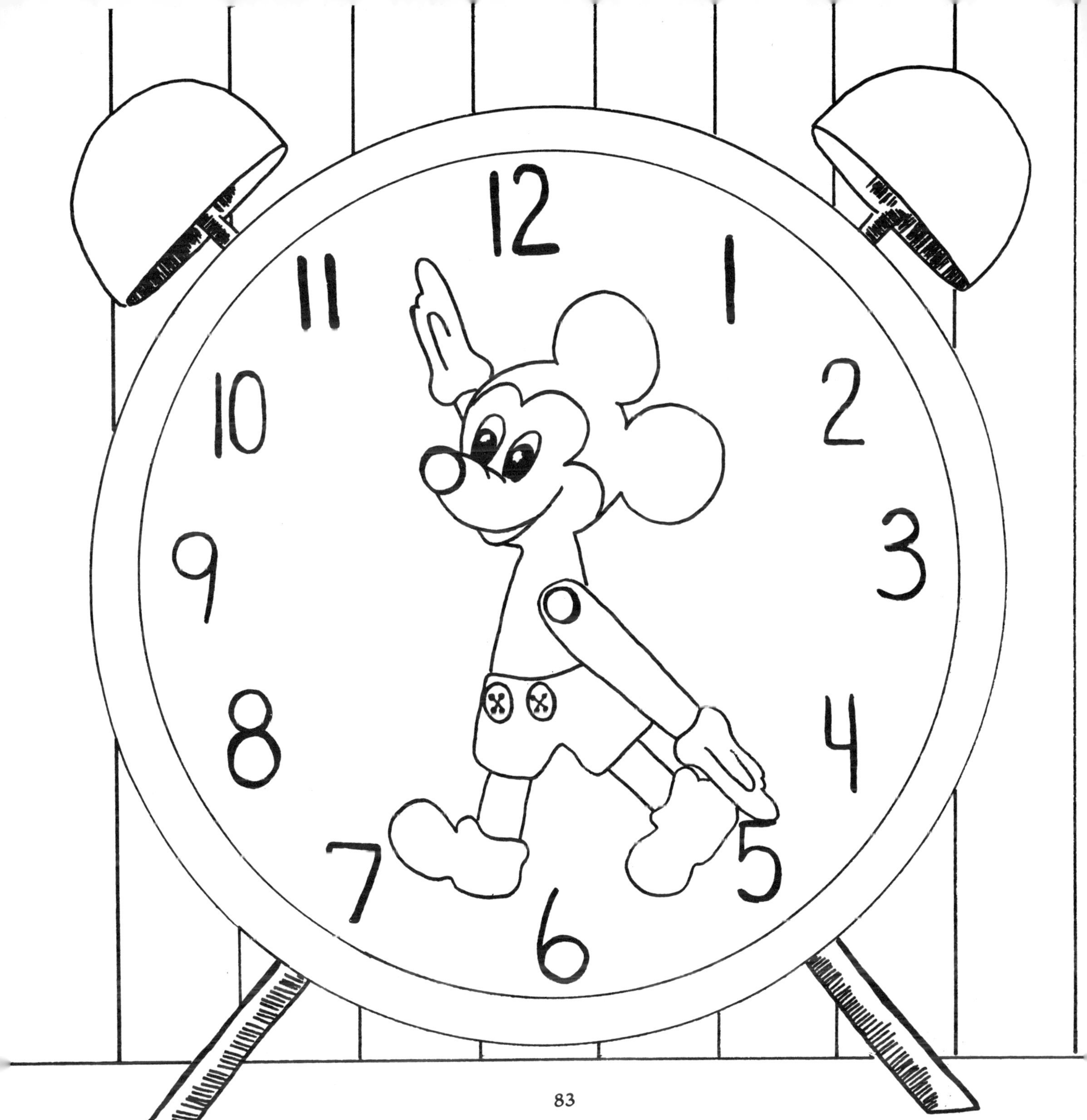
12
1
2
3
4
5
6
7
8
9
10
11

THE STUFF KIDS LOVE

What do kids **really** like? We asked a few of our friends for their favorites and found that some things never change.

Pizza is still the unanimous choice, with hamburgers and hot dogs close behind. Other vote-getters include lasagna, ice cream and Mexican fare. And not surprisingly, kids like foods that are fun to eat like our Icy Igloos, Animal Sandwiches and Banana Pops.

We've offered some new variations on kids favorites as well as some novel ideas for nutritious snacks for the next slumber party, late-night study session or bedtime story.

Any leftovers are sure to be a welcome addition to tomorrow's lunch box.

POPCORN NUT MIX

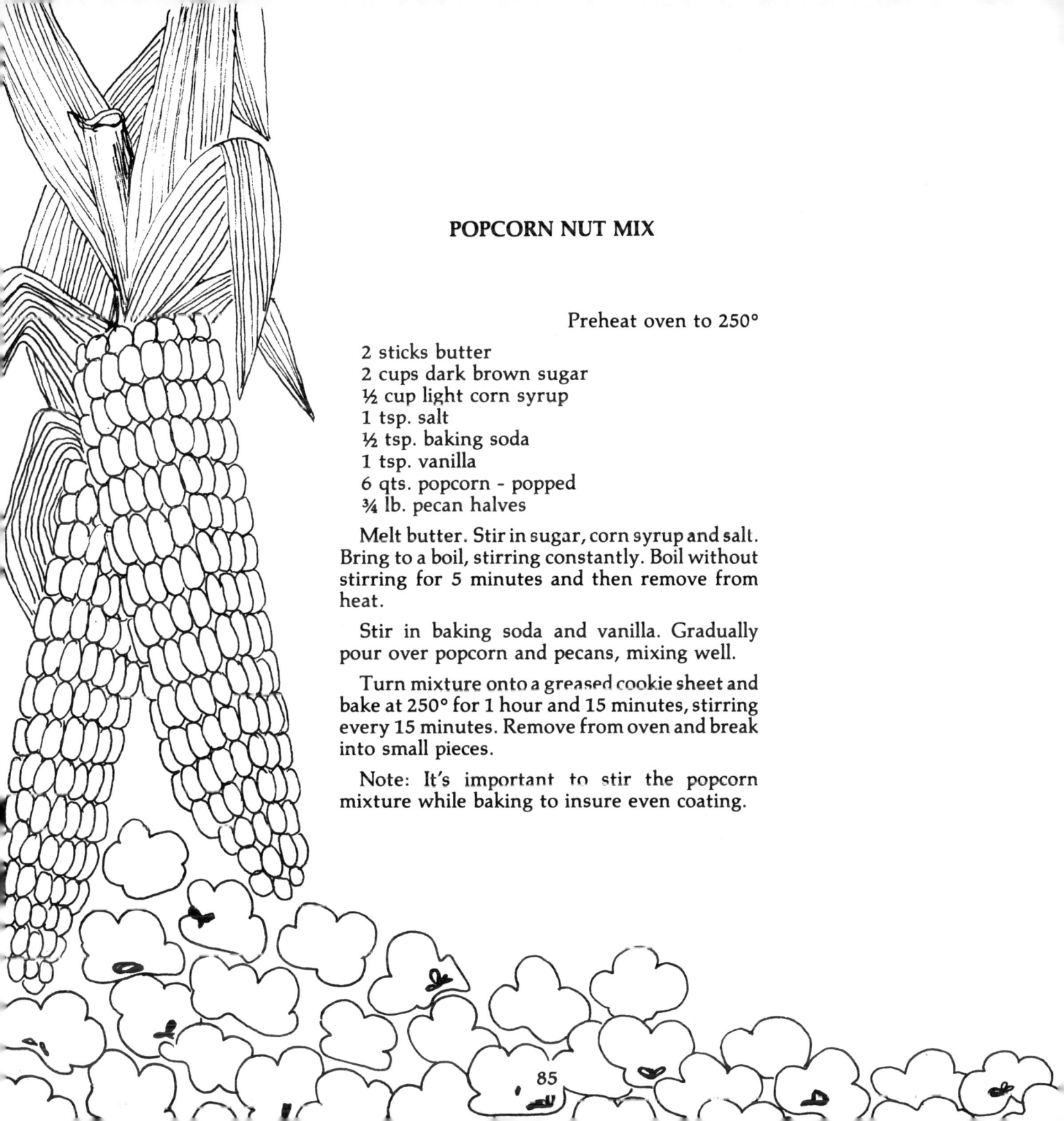

Preheat oven to 250°

2 sticks butter
2 cups dark brown sugar
½ cup light corn syrup
1 tsp. salt
½ tsp. baking soda
1 tsp. vanilla
6 qts. popcorn - popped
¾ lb. pecan halves

Melt butter. Stir in sugar, corn syrup and salt. Bring to a boil, stirring constantly. Boil without stirring for 5 minutes and then remove from heat.

Stir in baking soda and vanilla. Gradually pour over popcorn and pecans, mixing well.

Turn mixture onto a greased cookie sheet and bake at 250° for 1 hour and 15 minutes, stirring every 15 minutes. Remove from oven and break into small pieces.

Note: It's important to stir the popcorn mixture while baking to insure even coating.

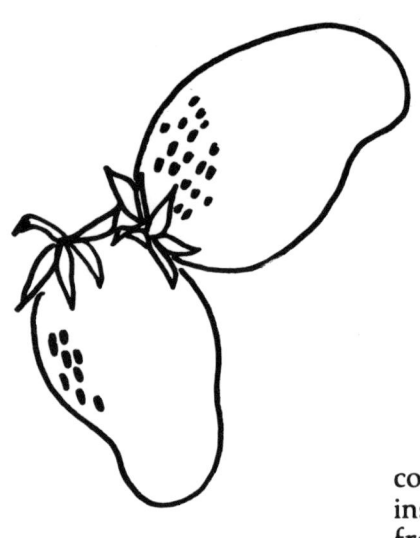

FROSTY STRAWBERRY LOLLIPOPS

Mix:

2 cups of pureed strawberries (or any other fruit - you can even use baby food fruit!)
1 cup orange, pineapple or apple juice
2 T. sugar (more or less to taste)

Freeze mixture in an ice cube tray with compartments. When mixture begins to freeze, insert a wooden ice cream stick. Return to freezer and serve when thoroughly hardened.

BANANA POPS

Peel bananas and cut in half. Push a wooden skewer into each half lengthwise. Freeze until well chilled. Dip into a mixture of melted chocolate (with a few drops of vegetable oil). Return to the freezer so chocolate hardens.

Instead of dipping in chocolate, you can brush the frozen banana with lemon juice and roll in coconut or sesame seeds. Then return to the freezer.

STRAWBERRY SODA

In a blender mix:
 1 T. strawberry gelatin
 2 T. very hot water
until the gelatin dissolves. Add 1 cup of milk and blend. Pour into a glass and add 3 scoops of vanilla ice cream. Serve with a straw.

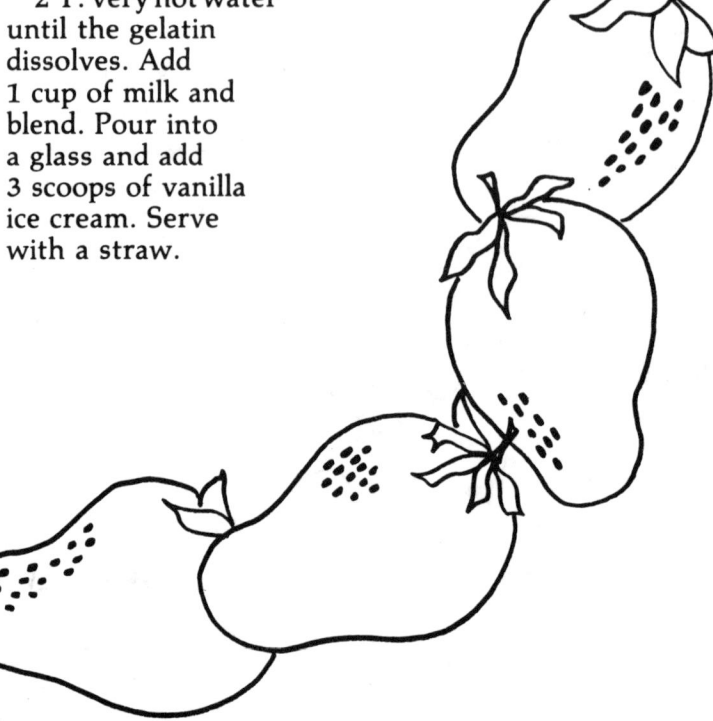

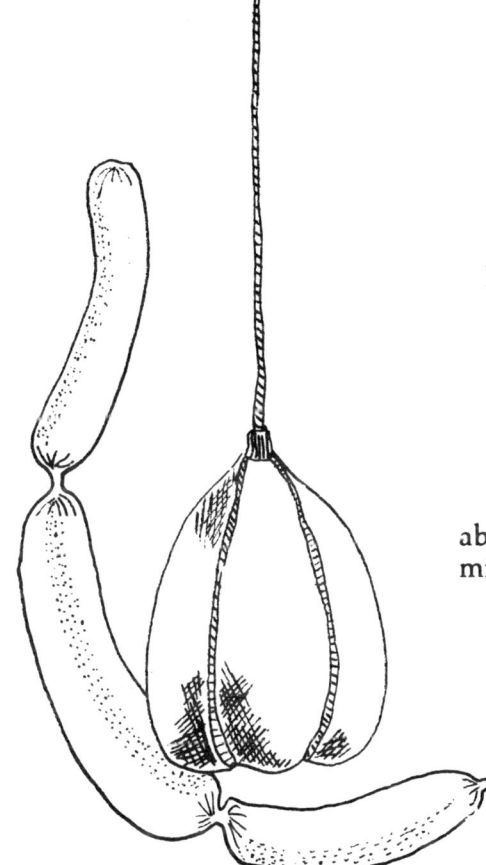

CHEESE STUFFED HOT DOG

Preheat oven to 350°

For each hot dog mix:

    3 T. grated cheddar cheese
    1 T. catsup
    1 tsp. finely grated onion
    dash of oregano
    dash of Tabasco sauce (optional)

Slit the hot dog lengthwise, and stuff with the above mixture. Wrap in foil "tent style". Bake 10 minutes at 350°, until the cheese melts.

HOT DOG SKEWERS

On a short skewer, alternate the following:

    chunks of hot dogs
    green pepper squares
    pieces of onion
    chunks of pineapple
    quartered tomatoes

Brush the skewer lightly with barbeque sauce and broil until the hot dog is brown (about 3 minutes).

PIZZA BAGELS

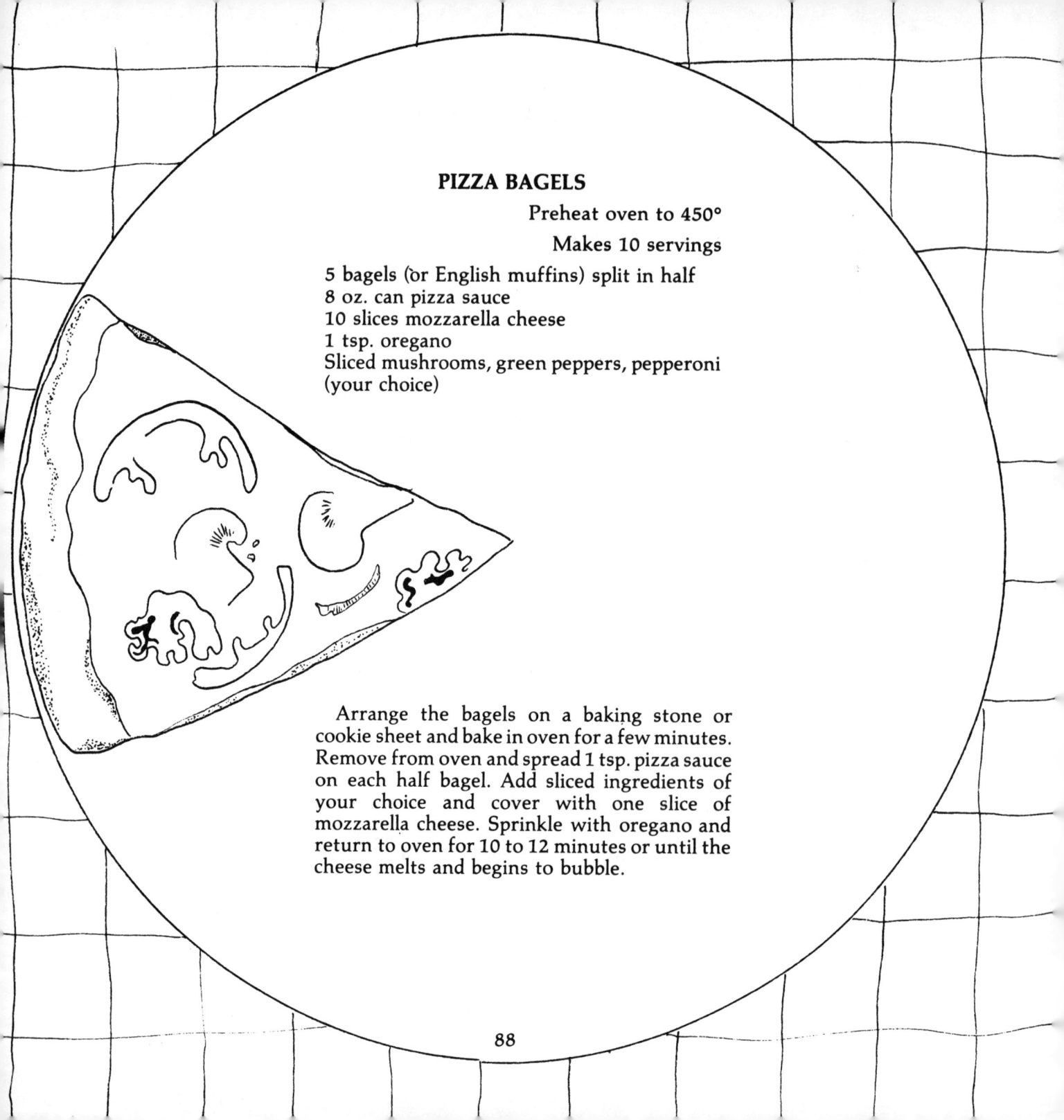

Preheat oven to 450°

Makes 10 servings

5 bagels (or English muffins) split in half
8 oz. can pizza sauce
10 slices mozzarella cheese
1 tsp. oregano
Sliced mushrooms, green peppers, pepperoni (your choice)

Arrange the bagels on a baking stone or cookie sheet and bake in oven for a few minutes. Remove from oven and spread 1 tsp. pizza sauce on each half bagel. Add sliced ingredients of your choice and cover with one slice of mozzarella cheese. Sprinkle with oregano and return to oven for 10 to 12 minutes or until the cheese melts and begins to bubble.

LASAGNA

Preheat oven to 350°

16 generous servings

Tomato Sauce (may be prepared the day before and refrigerated) (See p. 36)

1 cup chopped onion
2 tsp. minced garlic
2 T. olive oil
1 lb. ground beef
1 lb. bulk Italian sausage (or pork sausage)
2 6 oz. cans tomato paste
2 large cans Italian style tomatoes
2 8 oz. cans tomato sauce
1 T. sugar
1 T. oregano
1 T. basil
2 tsp. salt
1 bay leaf
dash of red pepper
1 T. Italian seasoning

Saute the onions and garlic in the oil. When onions are transparent, add the meat. Cook until the meat is brown. Drain. Add all of the remaining ingredients, stirring with a wooden spoon. Simmer 40 minutes, stirring often to prevent meat from sticking to the bottom of the pan and burning. Add ½ cup water if needed.

Other ingredients needed

1 box lasagna noodles, cooked according to package directions and drained
1 lb. ricotta cheese (can substitute cottage cheese if ricotta is not available)
½ cup parmesan cheese, grated

Begin building your lasagna by lightly oiling an 11" x 16" baking pan and lining pan with a layer of lasagna noodles. Spoon on a thin layer of sauce, a layer of mozzarella and dollops of ricotta or cottage cheese. Repeat until you have used all ingredients, ending with a layer of mozzarella cheese. Sprinkle the top with parmesan cheese.

Bake at 350° for 40 minutes. Let set for 10 minutes before cutting so it isn't "runny". Serve with garlic bread.

SLOPPY JOES

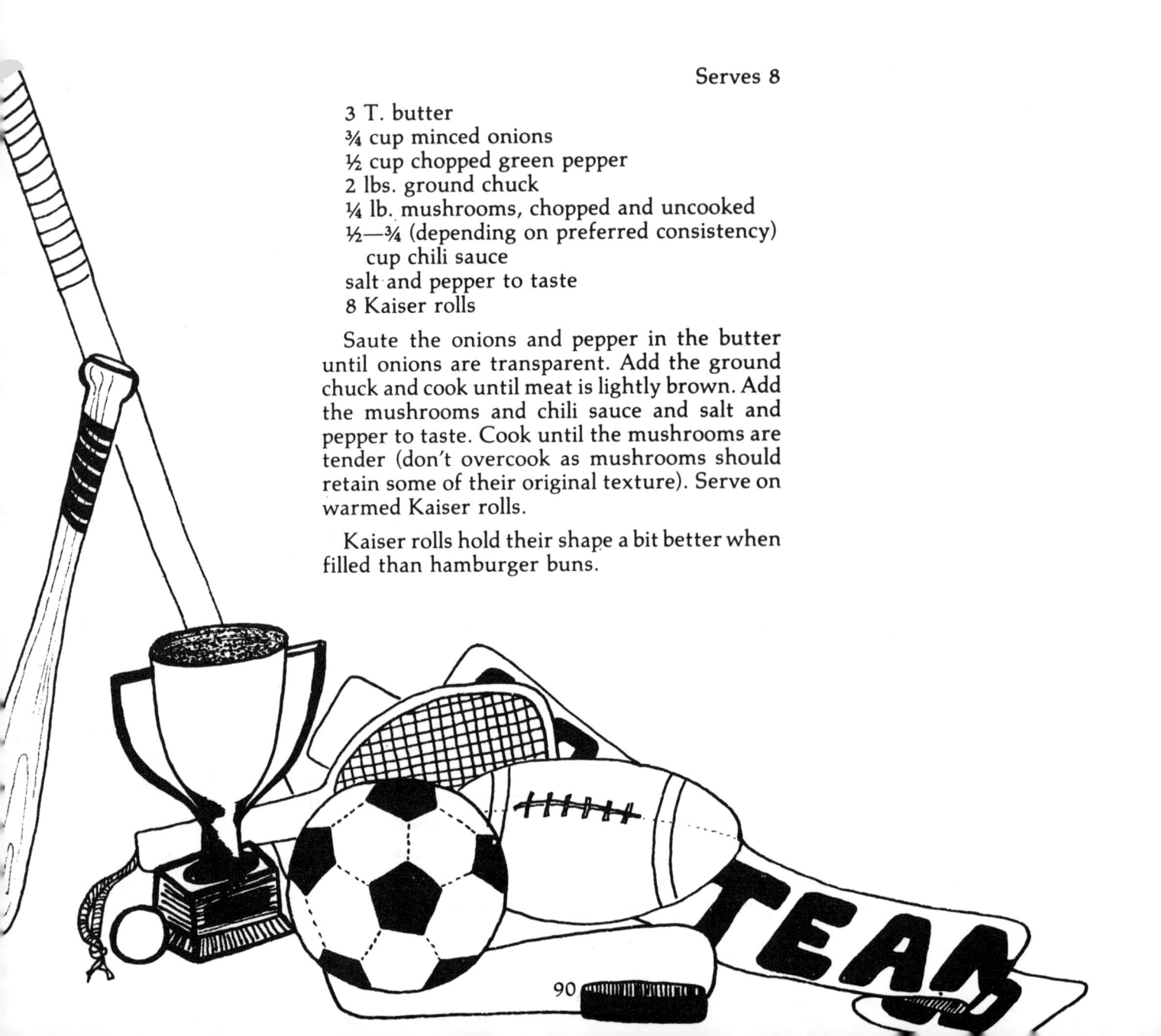

Serves 8

3 T. butter
¾ cup minced onions
½ cup chopped green pepper
2 lbs. ground chuck
¼ lb. mushrooms, chopped and uncooked
½—¾ (depending on preferred consistency) cup chili sauce
salt and pepper to taste
8 Kaiser rolls

Saute the onions and pepper in the butter until onions are transparent. Add the ground chuck and cook until meat is lightly brown. Add the mushrooms and chili sauce and salt and pepper to taste. Cook until the mushrooms are tender (don't overcook as mushrooms should retain some of their original texture). Serve on warmed Kaiser rolls.

Kaiser rolls hold their shape a bit better when filled than hamburger buns.

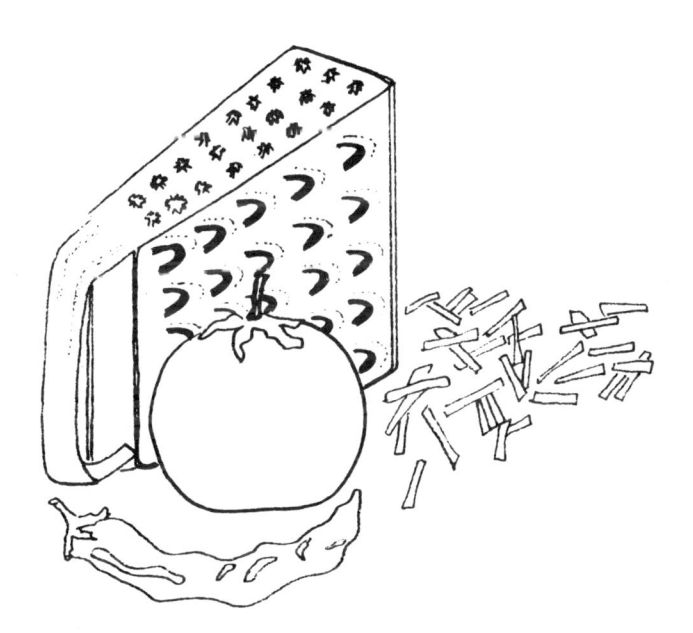

TACO TREATS - HOT and COLD

1 lb. lean ground beef
1 envelope taco seasoning mix
2 cups shredded cheddar cheese
3 chopped tomatoes
1 chopped avocado
2 medium onions, chopped
¼ head of lettuce, shredded
Thousand Island dressing

Brown the ground beef in a skillet until thoroughly cooked. Drain well. Add the envelope of seasoning mix and blend into the meat over low heat for about 1 minute. Remove from heat and cool.

Add the cheese, tomatoes, avocado, onions and lettuce to the cooled beef. Mix until well blended and moisten with Thousand Island dressing. Chill.

Place in a bowl and serve with corn and/or small tortilla chips that guests will use to "scoop up" the taco mixture.

For hot treats . . .

Brown the ground beef in a skillet, drain and add the taco seasoning mix. Return to the heat and add onions, cooking for another 3 minutes. Remove from heat and add cheese, tomatoes, and onions (omit lettuce and avocado). Blend with enough Thousand Island dressing to moisten.

Place the mixture on cocktail rye or small tortilla chips. Bake at 350° for about 10 minutes, until cheese melts. Serve (you may want to put a small dollop of sour cream on each piece before serving).

FAVORITE DOUGHNUTS

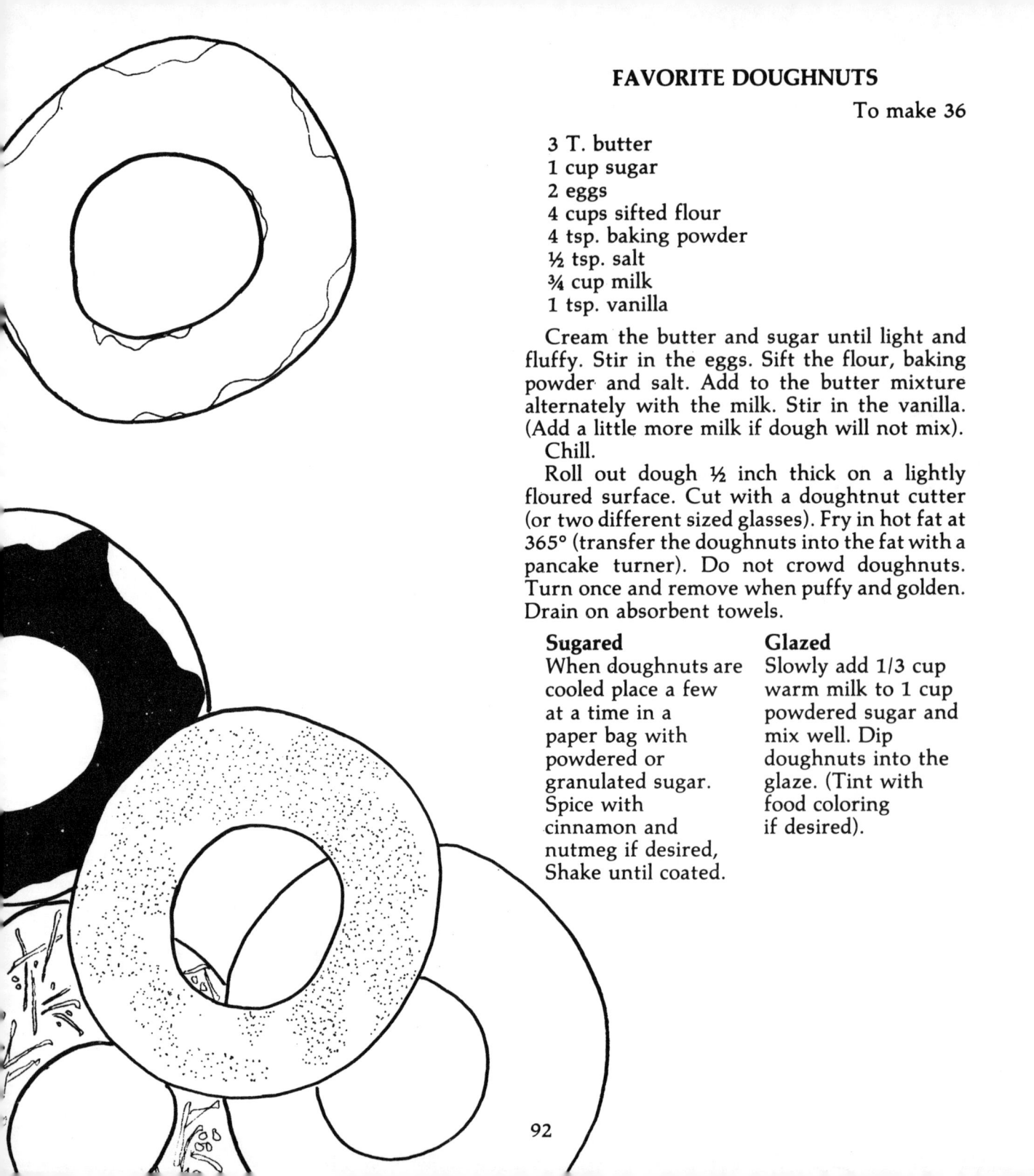

To make 36

3 T. butter
1 cup sugar
2 eggs
4 cups sifted flour
4 tsp. baking powder
½ tsp. salt
¾ cup milk
1 tsp. vanilla

Cream the butter and sugar until light and fluffy. Stir in the eggs. Sift the flour, baking powder and salt. Add to the butter mixture alternately with the milk. Stir in the vanilla. (Add a little more milk if dough will not mix). Chill.

Roll out dough ½ inch thick on a lightly floured surface. Cut with a doughnut cutter (or two different sized glasses). Fry in hot fat at 365° (transfer the doughnuts into the fat with a pancake turner). Do not crowd doughnuts. Turn once and remove when puffy and golden. Drain on absorbent towels.

Sugared
When doughnuts are cooled place a few at a time in a paper bag with powdered or granulated sugar. Spice with cinnamon and nutmeg if desired, Shake until coated.

Glazed
Slowly add 1/3 cup warm milk to 1 cup powdered sugar and mix well. Dip doughnuts into the glaze. (Tint with food coloring if desired).

ANIMAL SANDWICHES FOR TOTS

You will need:

a loaf of any kind of bread sliced lengthwise
a variety of sandwich fillings

Pink Elephants

Using an elephant cookie cutter, cut an elephant from the bread. Spread with deviled ham.
Use a slice of green olive for an eye.

Peter Rabbits

Combine a 3 oz. package of cream cheese with sliced green onions. Tint any color. Spread on a slice of bread. Cut out with a rabbit cutter and use a radish slice for an eye and celery strands for whiskers. Serve with a basket of hard boiled eggs, and "Stuffed Rabbit Sticks" p. 19.

Luscious Lions

Cut lions from the bread slice. Spread with peanut butter. Use raisins for the eyes and strings of celery for the whiskers.

Using a cake decorator, pipe the name of each child on the sandwich with softened cream cheese, either left white or tinted with food coloring.

Noah's Ark

Cut **two** of any animal desired. Spread filling on one slice and place a "top" on your animal sandwich. Wrap in plastic wrap and chill with a plate on top.

Hollow out a long loaf of Vienna or Rye Bread (For the "ark"). When sandwiches are well-chilled, remove plastic wrap and stand them up in the ark - make two of each animal!

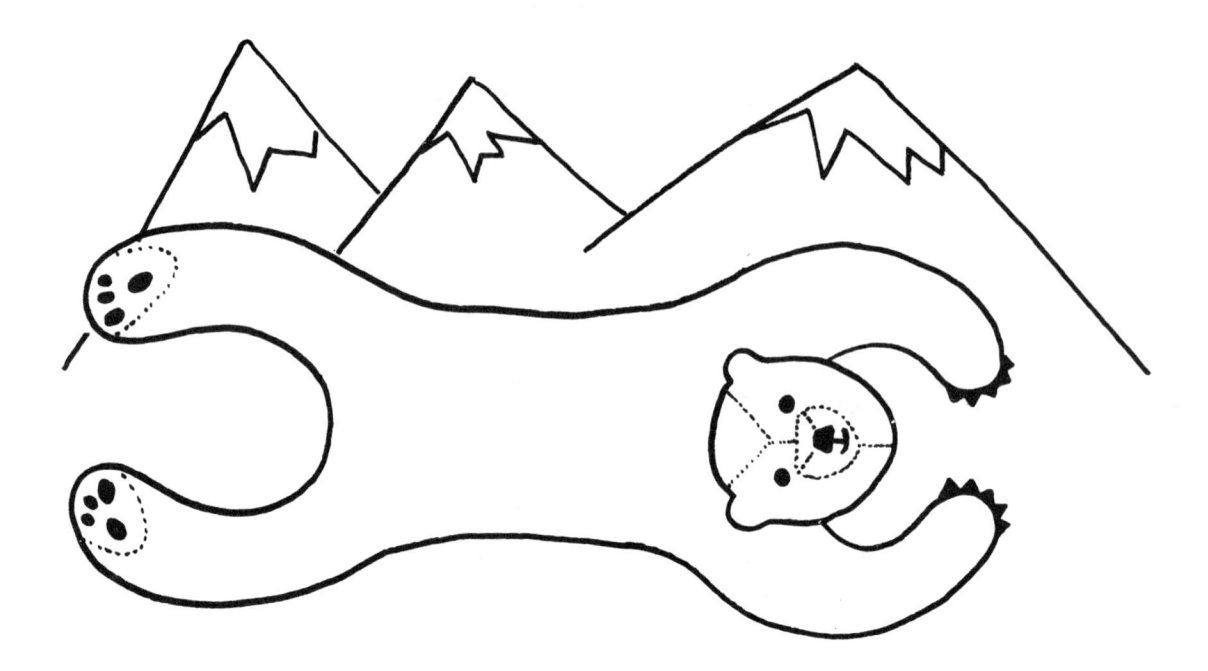

ICY IGLOOS

For 6 igloos   Preheat oven to 450°

6 packaged shortcake shells or 6 pieces of a one-layer cake, cut into rounds

6 scoops of very hard ice cream, your favorite flavor

Meringue

To make Meringue

4 egg whites at room temperature (but separate eggs when they are cold)
¼ tsp. salt
¼ cup sifted confectioners' sugar
¼ tsp. vanilla

Place egg whites and the salt in a large bowl and beat to a soft foam. Add the confectioners' sugar gradually, while beating. Add vanilla and continue beating until the meringue stands in peaks (it should be very stiff).

Cover a cookie sheet with brown paper and place the cakes on the cookie sheet. Top each cake with a scoop of ice cream. Cover the ice cream and cake completely with the meringue - make sure the ice cream and cake are sealed well.

Place in the hot oven for 5 minutes. Watch them carefully. Serve at once, as soon as the meringue tips brown.

If you prefer a "cold" igloo, you may spread the ice cream and cake completely with whipped cream and cover with coconut. Do not bake. Serve immediately.

7 Layer Cookies
Super easy and everyone's favorite!

Preheat oven to 350°

1 stick butter
1½ cups graham cracker crumbs
1 6 oz. package chocolate chips
1 6 oz. package butterscotch chips
1 5 oz. package coconut
1 14 oz. can sweetened condensed milk
1 cup chopped walnuts or pecans

Melt butter and pour in a 13" x 9" pan. Sprinkle graham cracker crumbs evenly over the butter. Sprinkle the chocolate and butterscotch chips over the crumbs. Drizzle the sweetened condensed milk over the chips so it is distributed evenly.

Cover the top with the coconut and nuts.

Bake for 30 minutes.

Cut into very small squares as one piece is very rich. These are best if kept in the refrigerator in an air tight container.

CHILI CON QUESO (Mexican Dip)

2 T. butter
1 medium onion
4 Jalapeno peppers, seeded and chopped very fine* OR 4 green chilis (canned) adding more if you wish a spicier dip
2 cups Monterrey Jack cheese, shredded
1 8 oz. package pasteurized American cheese food (e.g. Velvetta)
1 large tomato, peeled, chopped and drained
dash of cumin
dash of cayenne

Saute onions and peppers in butter until onions are transparent. Add the cheeses. Stir with a wooden spoon until melted and thoroughly blended. Add tomato and spices, blend and remove from heat.

Serve from a fondue pot or chafing dish with tortilla or corn chips.

* When working with peppers, wear rubber gloves and be careful not to touch your face. These peppers are very potent and leave a burning sensation.

NACHOS
Preheat oven to 350°

Easy as 1-2-3

1. Place desired amount of tortilla chips on foil on a cookie sheet
2. Sprinkle shredded Monterrey Jack or cheddar cheese over the chips. (Top with a Jalapeno or green chili pepper if desired).
3. Bake at 350° for 3 to 5 minutes, or until the cheese melts.

Serve with Salsa Picante (hot sauce) which is available in the Mexican food section of your grocery.

BACON, CHEESE AND TOMATO SANDWICHES

For each sandwich you will need:

1 slice white bread
2 slices American cheese
1 large tomato slice
2 slices partially cooked bacon

Toast the bread on one side. Spread the untoasted side with softened butter. Place a slice of American cheese on the buttered side of the bread. Add the tomato slice, and place the other cheese slice on top of the tomato. Top with 2 bacon slices. Broil until the cheese melts, and WATCH CAREFULLY. Cheese burns very fast!!

REUBEN SANDWICHES

For each sandwich you will need:

2 slices rye bread (only 1 slice if you
 prefer open-faced sandwiches)
1 T. butter
¼ lb. corned beef
½ cup sauerkraut (right from the can, drained)
1 slice Swiss cheese

Toast one side of the bread. Butter the untoasted side. Add the corned beef to the buttered side. Place sauerkraut on top of the corned beef and top with a slice of Swiss cheese. Place under the broiler until the cheese melts and the sauerkraut is warm. Remove from the broiler and serve open-faced or add the other slice of bread.

These can also be made with cocktail rye for "mini-sandwiches".

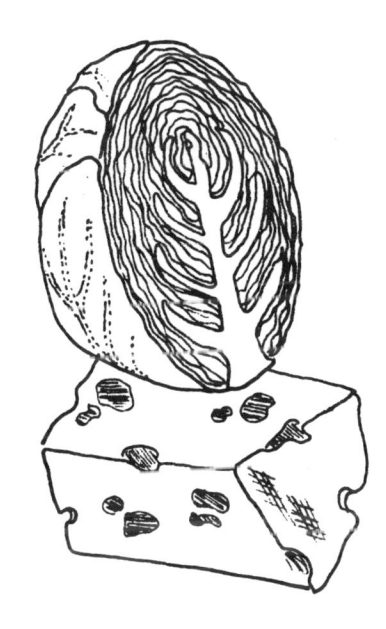

FOR LATE NIGHT STUDYING...

Trail Mix

Combine:
- ½ cup raisins
- ½ cup chopped nuts
- ¼ cup shredded coconut
- ½ cup dried apricots
- ½ cup banana chips

Store in a plastic bag for quick energy.

Fruity Milk Shake

Combine:
- ½ cup chilled fruit juice (apricot, strawberry, raspberry,
- 1 cup cold milk

Shake and serve over ice.

Chocolate Whip

- 4 oz. sweet chocolate
- 3 T. water
- 1 tsp. vanilla
- 1½ cups whipped cream
- ½ cup pecans

Heat the chocolate and water in a saucepan over low heat. Be careful that the chocolate doesn't get too hot. Remove from heat when chocolate has melted and cool. Add vanilla and fold in the whipped cream. Add nuts and pour into 4 wine glasses. Chill and eat!

INDEX

- A -
Almond Mushrooms 41
Animal Sandwiches for Tots 93
Apricot Coconut Balls 79
Artichokes Parmesano 54
Aunt Gen's Shrimp Dip 43
Avocado Boats 35

- B -
Bacon, Cheese & Tomato
   Sandwiches 97
Bacon Pecan Spread 50
Bacon Puffs 50
Banana Pops 86
BEEF
   Cocktail Meatballs 51
   Sloppy Joes 90
   Steak Tartare 48
   Taco Treats 91
Blender Gazpacho 12
Brandied Almonds 81
BREADS
   Cinnamon French Toast 59
   Don't Give Me Any Bologna ... 11
   Pizza Bagels 88
Sandwich Suggestions 11
Tomato Bread 29

- C -
Canine Chews 24
Canned Soup Wizardry 20
Cheddar Cheese Soup 28
Cheddar Puffs 53
CHEESE
   Artichokes Parmesano 54
   Bacon Pecan Spread 50
   Cheddar Cheese Soup 28
   Cheddar Balls 53
   Cheddar Puffs 53
   Cheese Stuffed Hot Dogs 87
   Cheese Topped Brussels Sprouts . 53
   Chili Con Queso 96
   Cider Cheese Crock 53
   Cocktail Cream Puffs 45
   Garlic Shrimp Fondue 49
   Nachos 96
   Olive Cheese Rounds 46
   Peter Rabbits 93
   Pizza Bagels 88
   Sesame Cheese Rounds 15
   Stuffed Baked Potato AuGratin 38
   Stuffed Cherry Tomatoes 44
   Stuffed Rabbit Sticks 19
   Tomato Bread 29

Cheese Stuffed Hot Dog 87
Cheese Topped Brussels Sprouts . 53
Cherries Jubilee 71
CHICKEN
   Chicken Divan Crepes 55
   Cocktail Cream Puffs 45
   Chicken Liver Pate with Curry 34
   Rumaki 32
   Salad Concoctions 16
   Chicken Salad Orientals 16
   Chicken Salad ala Orange 17
   Grace's Chicken Salad 17
   Quick & Easy 16
Chicken Divan Crepes 55
Chicken Salad Concoctions 16
Chili Con Queso 96
Chinese Orange Rolls 67
CHOCOLATE
   Chocolate Dessert Waffles 76
   Chocolate Whip 98
   Easy Fudge 75
   Homemade Chocolate Sauce ... 76
   Mandarin Orange Chocolate
     Sauce 77
   Seven Layer Cookies 95
   Tijuana Chocolate 68
Cider Cheese Crock 53
Cinnamon French Toast 59
Cocktail Cream Puffs 45
Cocktail Meatballs 51
Coffee Royal 68
Crabmeat ala Nancy 31
CREPES
   Chicken Divan 55
   Dessert 72

- D -
DESSERTS
   Apricot Coconut Balls 79
   Cherries Jubilee 71
   Chocolate Dessert Waffles 76
   Chocolate Whip 98
   Chinese Orange Rolls 67
   Hawaiian Pie 78
   Ice Cream Topping for One ... 22
   Icy Igloos 94
   Meringue Nut Kisses 80
   Peanut Butter Balls 82
   Peanut Butter Mallows 82
   Rum Logs 80
   Seven Layer Cookies 95
   Strawberries Elegante 74
   Toffee Torte 80

Dessert Crepes 72
DRINKS
   Daiquiri Frosts 27
   Fruity Milkshake 98
   Hot Buttered Rum 27
   Kir 27
   Strawberry Soda 86
   Spiked & Spiced Coffees 68
   Vinchaud 27

- E -
Easy Fudge 75
EGGS
   Bacon Puffs 50
   Huevos Rancheros 60
   Italian Omelette 61
   Garden Quiche 64
Escargot in Garlic Butter 33

- F -
Favorite Doughnuts 92
Fettucini Alfredo 30
Frosty Lollipops 86
Frosty Fruit Compote 66
FRUITS
   Apricot Coconut Balls 79
   Avocado Boats 35
   Banana Pops 86
   Cherries Jubilee 71
   Chicken Salad ala Orange 16
   Chinese Orange Rolls 67
   Frosty Fruit Compote 66
   Frosty Strawberry Lollipops ... 86
   Fruit Ambrosia 23
   Fruity Milkshake 98
   Gingered Pears 23
   Glazed Fruit Skewers 66
   Hawaiian Pie 78
   Mandarin Orange Chocolate
     Sauce 77
   Orange Syrup 62
   Pancakes ala Orange 62
   Strawberries Elegante 74
   Strawberry Soda 86
   Trail Mix 98
   Tutti Fruitti 23
     Banana Boats 23
     Spiced Oranges 23

- G -
Garden Quiche 64
Garlic Shrimp Fondue 49
Glazed Fruit Skewers 66

- H -

- Hawaiian Pie 78
- Hot Crabmeat Dip 31
- HOT DOGS
  - Cheese Stuffed Hot Dogs 87
  - Hot Dog Skewers 87
- Huevos Rancheros 60

- I -

- Ice Cream Toppings for One 22
- Icy Igloos 94
- Italian Omelette 61

- L -

- Lasagna 89

- M -

- Mandarin Orange Chocolate Sauce 77
- Meringue Nut Kisses 80
- Minestrone 52
- MUSHROOMS
  - Almond Mushrooms 41
  - Mushroom Turnovers 47
  - Pickled Fancy 42
  - Spinach Stuffed Mushrooms .. 41
- Mushroom Turnovers 47

- N -

- Nachos 96

- O -

- Olive Cheese Rounds 46

- P -

- Pancakes ala Orange 62
- Pancake Nonpareil 63
- PASTA
  - Fettucini Alfredo 30
  - Lasagna 89
  - Red Clam Sauce with Pasta Shells 36
  - Pate Brisee 64
- PEANUT BUTTER
  - Luscious Lions 93
  - Peanut Butter Balls 82
  - Peanut Butter Mallows 82
  - Suggestions for Using 13
- Pecan Waffles 63
- Pickled Fancy 42
- Pizza Bagels 88
- Popcorn Nut Mix 85

- R -

- Refried Beans 60
- Reubon Sandwich 97
- Rumaki 32
- Rumlogs 80

- S -

- Salmon Mousse with Dill Sauce .. 65
- SANDWICHES
  - Animal Sandwiches for Tots .. 93
  - Bacon, Cheese & Tomato 97
  - Have You Ever Tried Peanut Butter? 13
  - Reuben 97
  - Sloppy Joes 90
  - Suggestions 11
- SAUCES
  - Butterscotch 22
  - Curry 18
  - Dill 65
  - Garlic 18
  - Homemade Chocolate 76
  - Homemade Tomato Sauce 36
  - Ice Cream Topping 22
  - Mandarin Orange Chocolate .. 77
  - Orange Syrup 62
  - Raspberry 22
  - Red Clam Sauce 36
  - Salsa Picante 60
  - Snappy Tomato 18
- Seafood Bisques 14
- SEAFOOD & SHELLFISH
  - Aunt Gen's Shrimp Dip 43
  - Avocado Boats 35
  - Cocktail Cream Puffs (Anchovy) 45
  - Crabmeat ala Nancy 31
  - Escargot in Garlic Butter 33
  - Garlic Shrimp Fondue 49
  - Hot Crabmeat Dip 31
  - Salmon Mousse with Dill Sauce 65
  - Seafood Bisques 14
  - Shanghai Shrimp 37
  - Stuffed Baked Potato with Shrimp Sauce 38
- Sesame Cheese Rounds 15
- Seven Layer Cookies 95
- Shanghai Shrimp 37
- Sloppy Joes 90

- S -

- SOUPS
  - Bacon Clam 20
- Blender Gazpacho 12
- Cheddar Cheese 28
- Chicken Corn Chowder 20
- Chinese Egg Drop 20
- Cold Asparagus 20
- Creamiest Chicken Noodle 20
- Minestrone 52
- Scotch Pea 20
- Seafood Bisques 14
- Shrimp Newberg 20
- Soup Garnishes 21
- Spiced Nuts 81
- Spiced Oranges 23
- Spiked & Spiced Coffees 68
- Spinach Stuffed Mushrooms 41
- Steak Tartare 48
- Strawberries Elegante 74
- Strawberry Soda 86
- Stuffed Baked Potatoes 38
- Stuffed Cherry Tomatoes 44
- Stuffed Cucumbers 44
- Stuffed Rabbit Sticks 19

- T -

- Taco Treats 91
- Tijuana Chocolate 68
- Toffee Torte 80
- Tomato Bread 29
- Trail Mix 98

- V -

- VEGETABLES
  - Almond Mushrooms 41
  - Artichokes Parmesana 54
  - Blender Gazpacho 12
  - Cheese Topped Brussels Sprouts 53
  - Chicken Divan Crepes (Broccoli) 55
  - Garden Quiche 64
  - Minestrone 52
  - Mushroom Turnovers 47
  - Pickled Fancy 42
  - Spinach Stuffed Mushrooms .. 41
  - Stuffed Baked Potato with Seafood Sauce or AuGratin 38
  - Stuffed Cherry Tomatoes 44
  - Stuffed Cucumber 44
  - Stuffed Rabbit Sticks 19
  - Tomato Bread 29

- W -

- WAFFLES
  - Chocolate Dessert 76
  - Pecan 63
  - Toppings 63

INDEX

- A -
Almond Mushrooms 41
Animal Sandwiches for Tots 93
Apricot Coconut Balls 79
Artichokes Parmesano 54
Aunt Gen's Shrimp Dip 43
Avocado Boats 35

- B -
Bacon, Cheese & Tomato
   Sandwiches 97
Bacon Pecan Spread 50
Bacon Puffs 50
Banana Pops 86

BEEF
   Cocktail Meatballs 51
   Sloppy Joes 90
   Steak Tartare 48
   Taco Treats 91

Blender Gazpacho 12
Brandied Almonds 81

BREADS
   Cinnamon French Toast 59
   Don't Give Me Any Bologna .. 11
   Pizza Bagels 88

Sandwich Suggestions 11
Tomato Bread 29

- C -
Canine Chews 24
Canned Soup Wizardry 20
Cheddar Cheese Soup 28
Cheddar Puffs 53

CHEESE
   Artichokes Parmesano 54
   Bacon Pecan Spread 50
   Cheddar Cheese Soup 28
   Cheddar Balls 53
   Cheddar Puffs 53
   Cheese Stuffed Hot Dogs 87
   Cheese Topped Brussels Sprouts . 53
   Chili Con Queso 96
   Cider Cheese Crock 53
   Cocktail Cream Puffs 45
   Garlic Shrimp Fondue 49
   Nachos 96
   Olive Cheese Rounds 46
   Peter Rabbits 93
   Pizza Bagels 88
   Sesame Cheese Rounds 15
   Stuffed Baked Potato AuGratin 38
   Stuffed Cherry Tomatoes 44
   Stuffed Rabbit Sticks 19
   Tomato Bread 29

Cheese Stuffed Hot Dog 87
Cheese Topped Brussels Sprouts . 53
Cherries Jubilee 71

CHICKEN
   Chicken Divan Crepes 55
   Cocktail Cream Puffs 45
   Chicken Liver Pate with Curry 34
   Rumaki 32
   Salad Concoctions 16
   Chicken Salad Orientals 16
   Chicken Salad ala Orange 17
   Grace's Chicken Salad 17
   Quick & Easy 16

Chicken Divan Crepes 55
Chicken Salad Concoctions 16
Chili Con Queso 96
Chinese Orange Rolls 67

CHOCOLATE
   Chocolate Dessert Waffles 76
   Chocolate Whip 98
   Easy Fudge 75
   Homemade Chocolate Sauce ... 76
   Mandarin Orange Chocolate
      Sauce 77
   Seven Layer Cookies 95
   Tijuana Chocolate 68

Cider Cheese Crock 53
Cinnamon French Toast 59
Cocktail Cream Puffs 45
Cocktail Meatballs 51
Coffee Royal 68
Crabmeat ala Nancy 31

CREPES
   Chicken Divan 55
   Dessert 72

- D -
DESSERTS
   Apricot Coconut Balls 79
   Cherries Jubilee 71
   Chocolate Dessert Waffles 76
   Chocolate Whip 98
   Chinese Orange Rolls 67
   Hawaiian Pie 78
   Ice Cream Topping for One ... 22
   Icy Igloos 94
   Meringue Nut Kisses 80
   Peanut Butter Balls 82
   Peanut Butter Mallows 82
   Rum Logs 80
   Seven Layer Cookies 95
   Strawberries Elegante 74
   Toffee Torte 80

Dessert Crepes 72

DRINKS
   Daiquiri Frosts 27
   Fruity Milkshake 98
   Hot Buttered Rum 27
   Kir 27
   Strawberry Soda 86
   Spiked & Spiced Coffees 68
   Vinchaud 27

- E -
Easy Fudge 75

EGGS
   Bacon Puffs 50
   Huevos Rancheros 60
   Italian Omelette 61
   Garden Quiche 64

Escargot in Garlic Butter 33

- F -
Favorite Doughnuts 92
Fettucini Alfredo 30
Frosty Lollipops 86
Frosty Fruit Compote 66

FRUITS
   Apricot Coconut Balls 79
   Avocado Boats 35
   Banana Pops 86
   Cherries Jubilee 71
   Chicken Salad ala Orange 16
   Chinese Orange Rolls 67
   Frosty Fruit Compote 66
   Frosty Strawberry Lollipops ... 86
   Fruit Ambrosia 23
   Fruity Milkshake 98
   Gingered Pears 23
   Glazed Fruit Skewers 66
   Hawaiian Pie 78
   Mandarin Orange Chocolate
      Sauce 77
   Orange Syrup 62
   Pancakes ala Orange 62
   Strawberries Elegante 74
   Strawberry Soda 86
   Trail Mix 98
   Tutti Fruitti 23
      Banana Boats 23
      Spiced Oranges 23

- G -
Garden Quiche 64
Garlic Shrimp Fondue 49
Glazed Fruit Skewers 66

- H -

Hawaiian Pie 78
Hot Crabmeat Dip 31
HOT DOGS
    Cheese Stuffed Hot Dogs 87
    Hot Dog Skewers 87
Huevos Rancheros 60

- I -

Ice Cream Toppings for One 22
Icy Igloos 94
Italian Omelette 61

- L -

Lasagna 89

- M -

Mandarin Orange Chocolate Sauce 77
Meringue Nut Kisses 80
Minestrone 52
MUSHROOMS
    Almond Mushrooms 41
    Mushroom Turnovers 47
    Pickled Fancy 42
    Spinach Stuffed Mushrooms .. 41
Mushroom Turnovers 47

- N -

Nachos 96

- O -

Olive Cheese Rounds 46

- P -

Pancakes ala Orange 62
Pancake Nonpareil 63
PASTA
    Fettucini Alfredo 30
    Lasagna 89
    Red Clam Sauce with Pasta
      Shells 36
    Pate Brisee 64
PEANUT BUTTER
    Luscious Lions 93
    Peanut Butter Balls 82
    Peanut Butter Mallows 82
    Suggestions for Using 13
Pecan Waffles 63
Pickled Fancy 42
Pizza Bagels 88
Popcorn Nut Mix 85

- R -

Refried Beans 60
Reubon Sandwich 97
Rumaki 32
Rumlogs 80

- S -

Salmon Mousse with Dill Sauce .. 65
SANDWICHES
    Animal Sandwiches for Tots .. 93
    Bacon, Cheese & Tomato 97
    Have You Ever Tried
      Peanut Butter? 13
    Reuben 97
    Sloppy Joes 90
    Suggestions 11
SAUCES
    Butterscotch 22
    Curry 18
    Dill 65
    Garlic 18
    Homemade Chocolate 76
    Homemade Tomato Sauce 36
    Ice Cream Topping 22
    Mandarin Orange Chocolate .. 77
    Orange Syrup 62
    Raspberry 22
    Red Clam Sauce 36
    Salsa Picante 60
    Snappy Tomato 18
Seafood Bisques 14
SEAFOOD & SHELLFISH
    Aunt Gen's Shrimp Dip 43
    Avocado Boats 35
    Cocktail Cream Puffs (Anchovy) 45
    Crabmeat ala Nancy 31
    Escargot in Garlic Butter 33
    Garlic Shrimp Fondue 49
    Hot Crabmeat Dip 31
    Salmon Mousse with Dill Sauce 65
    Seafood Bisques 14
    Shanghai Shrimp 37
    Stuffed Baked Potato with Shrimp
      Sauce 38
Sesame Cheese Rounds 15
Seven Layer Cookies 95
Shanghai Shrimp 37
Sloppy Joes 90

- S -

SOUPS
    Bacon Clam 20

Blender Gazpacho 12
Cheddar Cheese 28
Chicken Corn Chowder 20
Chinese Egg Drop 20
Cold Asparagus 20
Creamiest Chicken Noodle 20
Minestrone 52
Scotch Pea 20
Seafood Bisques 14
Shrimp Newberg 20
Soup Garnishes 21
Spiced Nuts 81
Spiced Oranges 23
Spiked & Spiced Coffees 68
Spinach Stuffed Mushrooms 41
Steak Tartare 48
Strawberries Elegante 74
Strawberry Soda 86
Stuffed Baked Potatoes 38
Stuffed Cherry Tomatoes 44
Stuffed Cucumbers 44
Stuffed Rabbit Sticks 19

- T -

Taco Treats 91
Tijuana Chocolate 68
Toffee Torte 80
Tomato Bread 29
Trail Mix 98

- V -

VEGETABLES
    Almond Mushrooms 41
    Artichokes Parmesana 54
    Blender Gazpacho 12
    Cheese Topped Brussels Sprouts 53
    Chicken Divan Crepes (Broccoli) 55
    Garden Quiche 64
    Minestrone 52
    Mushroom Turnovers 47
    Pickled Fancy 42
    Spinach Stuffed Mushrooms .. 41
    Stuffed Baked Potato with Seafood
      Sauce or AuGratin 38
    Stuffed Cherry Tomatoes 44
    Stuffed Cucumber 44
    Stuffed Rabbit Sticks 19
    Tomato Bread 29

- W -

WAFFLES
    Chocolate Dessert 76
    Pecan 63
    Toppings 63